The Bahá'í Religion

D1296352

By the same author

In Iran: Studies in Bábí and Bahá'í History, Vols. 3 and 5
The Babi and Baha'i Religions: From Messianic Shi'ism to a
   World Religion

The Bahá'í Religion

*A Short Introduction
to its
History and Teachings*

by

Peter Smith

297.89
5
ph
cat.

GEORGE RONALD
OXFORD

LAKEWOOD MEMORIAL LIBRARY
LAKEWOOD, NEW YORK 14750

GEORGE RONALD, Publisher
46 HIGH STREET, KIDLINGTON, OXFORD, OX5 2DN

© PETER SMITH 1988
All Rights Reserved

British Library Cataloguing in Publication Data

Smith, Peter, *1947 Nov. 27–*
  The Baha'i religion
  1. Bahaism
  I. Title
  297'.89

  ISBN 0–85398–277–5

Typeset by Photoprint, Torquay, Devon.
Printed and bound in Great Britain by
Richard Clay Ltd., Bungay, Suffolk.

Contents

Acknowledgements

IN writing this book I have incurred various debts of gratitude. First, then, let me thank Dr Iraj Ayman, formerly of the Bangkok Office of UNESCO, and Dr Pinit Ratanakul, Director of the Religious Studies Programme Mahidol University, for their original joint suggestion that I write this book, and for their subsequent enthusiastic encouragement. I must also thank various friends and colleagues for their encouragement and for their critical reading of the original manuscript. Amongst these let me offer my particular thanks to Juan Cole, Michael Fonner, Shirley Govindasamy, Stephen Lambden, Moojan Momen, Wendi Momen and Sammireh Smith.

Much of this book was first presented in a lecture course on the History of Religions which I delivered as part of the Religious Studies Programme at Mahidol University. In this connection, my thanks are due to several classes of graduate students in that Programme for their attentive questions, and in particular to Mr Narintorn Chimsuntorn who on occasion acted as my translator. My thanks also to the staff of both the Department of Humanities and the Institute of Language and Culture for Rural Development at Mahidol for their general help and assistance.

Special thanks must go to Miss Suthida Boontaksinapan and Miss Umpai Nulek who typed the successive versions of my manuscript, and to all those at George Ronald who worked to turn that manuscript into the present book.

As always I offer my particular thanks to my wife and children for their support and understanding during the period in which I was preparing this book.

Introduction

I

THIS book provides a brief introduction to the Bahá'í Faith. Now established in most of the countries of the world, Bahá'í represents a religious movement of considerable scope and dynamism. As such, it is of interest to anyone who is concerned with contemporary developments in religion.

Bahá'í centres on the person and teachings of Bahá'u'lláh (1817–92), a nineteenth-century Iranian who claimed to be the messenger of God for the present age. Regarded by his followers as the promised redeemer of all past religions, Bahá'u'lláh announced that he had come to establish a new world order in which the peoples and religions of the world would be united and live together in peace and harmony. For Bahá'ís, this millennial vision represents the ultimate goal of their activities. Whatever the sufferings of this present 'age of transition', they believe that human society – just as the human individual – can be transformed by the light of faith.

II

In writing this book for the general reader, I have sought to give a succinct account of the history, religious and social doctrines, ethics, practices and organization of the Bahá'í religion. An Appendix of short extracts from the Bahá'í writings has also been provided, and some suggestions for further reading are listed in the Bibliography.

In such a short book many issues of importance and interest have been left aside. Of the omissions, perhaps the most glaring is the lack of historical depth and context. Specifically, I have not written an intellectual history of Bahá'í beliefs and practices. Bahá'u'lláh is central to any study of Bahá'í religious tenets, but after him the Bahá'ís have had a succession of leaders – 'Abdu'l-Bahá, Shoghi Effendi and the Universal House of Justice – whom they regard as divinely guided. Authoritative Bahá'í writings, then, date from the mid-nineteenth century through to the present day and show various patterns of development and change. This complexity is here ignored, and I write generically of the teachings of the 'successive Baha'i leaders'. Again, I do not attempt to portray these teachings in the changing intellectual and social contexts of their times, and I generally present modern Bahá'í beliefs rather than reconstructing the belief structures of earlier generations of Bahá'ís.

III

There is invariably a measure of interpretation in any general account of a religious movement. Therefore, authors often notify their readers of their own personal position vis-à-vis the subject of their study. Let me note, then, that I am both a Bahá'í and a humanistically-inclined social scientist-cum-historian. I trust that my account is relatively free from such biases as may arise from either of these positions.

Peter Smith
Bangkok
September 1987

For Sammi, Corinne and James

Chronology

1844   The Báb's initial declaration of his mission in Shiraz (22/23 May).

1850   The Báb is publicly executed in Tabriz (9 July).

1852   Attempt on the life of the Shah (15 August). General persecution of the Bábís. Bahá'u'lláh is imprisoned in the Black Pit of Tehran.

1853–6 Bahá'u'lláh is exiled to Baghdad (arrives 8 April 1853), and then withdraws to the mountains of Kurdistan (1854–6).

1856–63 Bahá'u'lláh's increasing pre-eminence as a Bábí leader in Baghdad. Writes the *Hidden Words, Seven Valleys* and *Book of Certitude*.

1863   Bahá'u'lláh and his followers gather in the Riḍván garden (21 April – 2 May) and then travel to Istanbul and Edirne.

1865–8 Bahá'u'lláh's sojourn in Edirne (from December 1863). The division between Bahá'u'lláh and Ṣubḥ-i-Azal (Spring 1866) and the emergence of a distinct Bahá'í community. The beginning of Bahá'u'lláh's letters to the kings.

1868–92 Bahá'u'lláh's exile to 'Akká and its environs (from 31 August 1868). His composition of the *Most Holy Book* (c. 1873) and its supplementary works.

1892   Death of Bahá'u'lláh (29 May) and 'Abdu'l-Bahá's succession to leadership.

1910–13 'Abdu'l-Bahá's travels to Egypt, Europe and North America.

1921   Death of 'Abdu'l-Bahá (28 November). Shoghi Effendi is named as Guardian of the Cause (3 January 1922).

1957   Death of Shoghi Effendi (4 November). The Hands of the Cause assume supreme authority (25 November).

1963   First election of the Universal House of Justice (April).

1

The Emergence and Development of the Bahá'í Faith

CENTRAL to Bahá'í religious faith is the belief in the continuity of divine guidance to humankind. In every age there appears a messenger or 'Manifestation' of God who imparts both a reassertion of eternal religious truths, particular teachings appropriate to the present age, and a fresh measure of spiritualizing energy which enables humanity to progress further in God's eternal plan.

According to Bahá'í belief, the central religious figures of the present age are the Báb (1819–50), the founder of the short-lived Bábí religion; Bahá'u'lláh (1817–92), the founder of the Bahá'í Faith and the Manifestation of God for the present age; and 'Abdu'l-Bahá (1844–1921), Bahá'u'lláh's eldest son and his appointed successor and interpreter. For Bahá'ís, the lives and teachings of these three individuals provide both the basis for the development of a new world civilization and the means of salvation for our present distracted age. Together the ministries of these three men constitute the Bahá'í 'Heroic Age' (1844–1921), succeeded in turn by a 'Formative Age' (1921–), in which the new religion has undergone global expansion and developed its administrative order. In time, it is believed, this Formative Age will be succeeded by a 'Golden Age' in which Bahá'u'lláh's millennial 'new world order' will be established.

Changes in leadership divide the historical account into five main periods: early Bábism (1844–c. 1856); Bahá'u'lláh's transformation of Bábism and his subsequent establishment of the Bahá'í religion (c. 1856–92); and the periods of leadership of

LAKEWOOD MEMORIAL LIBRARY
LAKEWOOD, NEW YORK 14750

'Abdu'l-Bahá (1892–1921), Shoghi Effendi (1922–57), and the Universal House of Justice (1963 –).

The Bábí Religion (1844– *c.* 56)

The Bahá'í Faith emerged out of the Bábí movement, and retrospectively Bahá'ís have incorporated the earlier religion as an inherent part of their own.

Bábism itself was rooted in the world of nineteenth-century Iranian Shi'i Islam. A proper study of its history would require a discussion of these Islamic roots, but for reasons of brevity this is not attempted here. Suffice it to say that the Bábí religion began in 1844 as a messianic reform movement within Islam. At its centre was its youthful prophet, the merchant Siyyid 'Alí Muḥammad Shírází, who came to be known by his religious title of the *Báb* (the 'gate' to the messianic Hidden Imam). The Báb first announced the near advent of the Imam, and then later proclaimed that he himself was the Imam. He then attempted to promulgate a new system of holy law to replace Islamic holy law, thus implicitly originating a new religion.

Such actions were enormously controversial and provoked the fierce antagonism of many of the *'ulamá*, the Islamic learned who safeguarded orthodoxy. Nevertheless, the new religion spread quickly throughout Iran and attracted a wide range of followers, including some of considerable social prominence. Attempts to curtail the activities of the Bábí missionaries led to violence, and in 1848 there was a protracted armed struggle between a group of Bábís and their orthodox opponents. Government forces intervened and the Bábís were crushed. Persecution became more intense, and in several areas there was further fighting. In 1850 the Báb was executed. Many of his leading followers had already been killed, and the movement soon fragmented. The overall leadership of the movement passed to Mírzá Yaḥyá Núrí (1830/1–1912), known by his religious title of Ṣubḥ-i-Azal (Morn of Eternity), but his leadership was weak and ineffective. In 1852 one Bábí faction unsuccessfully attempted to assassinate the Shah. A general persecution followed, and those Bábís who survived were driven underground.

This collapse of the movement precluded the development of a fully developed religious system. The Báb had provided the basis for such a system, but his writings were not readily accessible; and with the death of most of the movement's early leaders, a plethora of rival claims to succession, and the constraints of persecution, no systematic and cohesive system could be developed. The Bábís had proclaimed the messianic fulfilment of Islam, but beyond that basic belief, the Bábí survivors remained largely within the conceptual world of Iranian Shi'ism. Aspects of Bábí religious doctrine and some religious practices were later incorporated into the Bahá'í Faith, but the Bábís' main legacy was their self-sacrificial enthusiasm and their conviction that God was fulfilling his promise of salvation. For Bahá'ís, the Bábís were 'God-intoxicated' heroes who struggled to establish the truth of God's cause and died as martyrs in its defence. The Báb and his followers were the heralds of the new age marked by the Bahá'í Revelation.

Bahá'u'lláh and the Establishment of the Bahá'í Religion (c. 1856–92)

The reanimation of the Bábí movement was largely the work of Mírzá Husayn 'Alí Núrí, who later became known by his religious title Bahá'u'lláh (the 'Glory' or 'Splendour' of God). Bahá'u'lláh was an older half-brother of Subh-i-Azal. His father, Mírzá 'Abbás (d. 1839) had been a rich and influential landowner and government official, but the son had interested himself in religious and charitable concerns rather than followed a political career. In 1844/5 he became a Bábí and had lent considerable support to the new movement. Along with other prominent Bábís, he had been imprisoned during the general persecution of 1852. After four months in the loathsome 'Black Pit' of Tehran he was released and forced into exile in Ottoman Iraq, establishing his residence in Baghdad.

Bahá'u'lláh was now evidently increasingly filled with a powerful religious vision, and he later described how in the midst of his sufferings in the Black Pit he had undergone profound mystical experiences in which God had promised to render him victorious. Subh-i-Azal had joined him in Baghdad, but his

young brother's style of leadership was not acceptable to
Bahá'u'lláh, and for two years (1854–6) he withdrew to live a
life of religious seclusion in the mountains of Kurdistan. Upon
his return to Baghdad in the spring of 1856, he increasingly came
to dominate the colony of Bábí exiles. Corresponding with the
Bábí remnant in Iran, and acting as a focal point for exiles and
travellers, he began to gradually revivify the Bábí movement.
Many Bábís became his disciples, disseminating ever more widely
his letters and other writings.

Fearing the re-emergence of Bábism, the Iranian government
petitioned the Ottoman authorities to remove Bahá'u'lláh from
the sensitive border province of Baghdad. Accordingly, he was
invited to proceed to Istanbul. On the eve of his departure for the
Ottoman capital, he stayed for twelve days (21 April – 2 May
1863) in the garden of Ridván (Rezván) on the outskirts of
Baghdad, meeting with his followers and friends. These twelve
days have assumed great importance, for although the exact
details of what occurred in the Ridván garden are not given in
contemporary sources, Bahá'ís believe that it was at Ridván that
Bahá'u'lláh first made known his full claim to divine authority.

After leaving Ridván, Bahá'u'lláh travelled to Istanbul with his
family and a number of followers and associates, and then, after a
few months, the entire party was exiled to Edirne (Adrianople) in
European Turkey. Ṣubḥ-i-Azal still remained the nominal head
of the movement, but during the years in Edirne (1863–8)
increasing tension developed between the two half-brothers.
Unable to provide unitary leadership to the Bábís, Azal
apparently resented his brother's growing pre-eminence. Consequently, in 1866 the exile community in Edirne split between
the followers of Ṣubḥ-i-Azal (the Azalís) and those of Bahá'u'lláh
(the Bahá'ís), with the Bahá'ís in the majority. Bahá'u'lláh now
made open claim to be a divine messenger and the promised one
foretold by the Báb, and dispatched emissaries to Iran to proclaim
his cause. Quite rapidly the majority of the Bábís became
Bahá'ís, albeit that the Iranian Azalís remained a significant
minority until the early years of this century. The year 1866 thus
marks the actual beginning of the Bahá'í Faith as a separate
religion.

In 1868 the Ottoman authorities again intervened. Aware of the split between the Bahá'ís and the Azalís, and wary of religious disputation and heterodoxy, they subjected both groups in Edirne to a further exile. Bahá'u'lláh and his entourage they sent to the prison of 'Akká (Acre) in Ottoman Syria. Azal was sent to Famagusta in Cyprus. Both leaders remained in or near their respective places of exile until the end of their lives.

It was during the period of Bahá'u'lláh's exile in Syria (1868–92) that the Bahá'í Faith was consolidated as a religious movement. Imprisoned in an obscure and distant city, Bahá'u'lláh's contact with his followers was necessarily limited to the exchange of correspondence and the arduous pilgrimages of his Iranian devotees to 'Akká. Gradually circumstances in 'Akká were eased. Thus, after two years of close confinement in the Citadel, he was placed under house arrest inside the city for a further seven years, and then finally allowed to live in the surrounding countryside, ending his days in the mansion of Bahjí. Even so, it was a formidable organizational challenge to coordinate the activities of the movement, and it was only through a network of Bahá'í couriers and representatives that effective consolidation was accomplished. These organizational tasks became predominantly the responsibility of Bahá'u'lláh's eldest son, 'Abbás ('Abdu'l-Bahá – 1844–1921), who in turn succeeded to the leadership of the movement after his father's death in 1892. Bahá'u'lláh, for his part, was able to spend these last twenty-four years of his life in writing, in instructing his followers and, after 1877, in the enjoyment of the countryside.

Bahá'u'lláh's writings now came to be regarded as direct revelations from God, a status that was also retrospectively applied to his writings prior to the declaration of his mission in Riḍván. The total corpus of this work is immense and, including letters, some 15,000 of Bahá'u'lláh's 'Tablets' have so far been collected. These range widely over many subjects but display a distinct progression in the concerns expressed during the course of his ministry. Thus, Bahá'u'lláh's earliest extant writings (c. 1852–6) comprise a number of exaltatory poems and a Quranic commentary, which were written basically within the Bábí tradition. It was only during the later Baghdad period (1856–63), that a distinctive message began to emerge. The nature of this message is shown characteristically in two books, both of which were widely circulated. In the first, *The Hidden Words (Kalimát-i Maknúnih*, 1857–8), Bahá'u'lláh emphasized the practical, moral and spiritual demands of man's relationship with God. In the second, *The Book of Certitude (Kitáb-i-Íqán*, 1862), he outlined in clear language the Bábí (Bahá'í) doctrine of prophetic succession (see pp. 15–17), assured his readers of the continuing bounty and guidance of God, and described the basic requirements for those who wish to become 'true seekers' after God.

During the Edirne period (1863–8), several new themes emerged, most prominently that of his own claim to divine authority. Apart from this, he began to prescribe the pattern of life which his followers should adopt, and prepared the first of a series of proclamatory letters to the rulers of the world in which he announced his mission and admonished them to work for justice and international conciliation. He also forbade religious militancy and instructed his followers to avoid sedition.

All these themes were continued during the 'Akká period (1868–92). Including the earlier epistles, proclamatory letters were sent to the rulers of the Ottoman Empire, Iran, Britain, Russia and France, as well as to the Pope (Pius IX) and to various Islamic religious leaders. In his *Most Holy Book (Kitáb-i-Aqdas*, c. 1873) and several supplementary writings, he detailed the main requirements of a distinctive code of Bahá'í religious law, thereby clearly differentiating his followers from both Bábís and Muslims. Finally, in a series of writings, he enunciated the major precepts and principles which were to distinguish his mission, such as in *Splendours (Ishráqat* – see Appendix).

'Abdu'l-Bahá (1844–1921)

Bahá'u'lláh appointed as his successor his eldest son, 'Abbás Effendi, now better known by his title 'Abdu'l-Bahá (the servant of Bahá). 'Abdu'l-Bahá's leadership was of major importance in the development of the Bahá'í religion. Although 'Abdu'l-Bahá emphasized that he was not a prophet of God like his father, he did claim to be divinely guided in his leadership and to be the authorized interpreter of his father's teachings. Thus, the principle of a single divinely-inspired leader was continued, and the doctrinal and organizational unity of the movement was emphasized and maintained. Correspondingly, opposition to that leadership — as exampled most particularly by the opposition of 'Abdu'l-Bahá's half-brothers — was severely censured. Such action was regarded as a violation of Bahá'u'lláh's Covenant with his followers, and those who thereby chose to become 'Covenant-breakers' were to be expelled from the Bahá'í community.

'Abdu'l-Bahá's role as the authorized interpreter of his father's teachings has further importance in that it led to a massive addition to the corpus of authoritative Bahá'í writings. 'Abdu'l-Bahá also stated Bahá'í positions on contemporary issues and introduced distinctive expressions of Bahá'í belief, as in the set of Bahá'í principles which he enunciated during the course of his Western journeys.

The period of 'Abdu'l-Bahá's leadership also witnessed a considerable change in the nature of the Bahá'í community. In Iran these years were a time of much social and political turmoil. In the midst of this the Bahá'í community increasingly emerged as a distinctive and self-confident religious community with its own publicly recognized institutions and principles. The neighbouring Bahá'í communities in Asiatic Russia and British India also became more buoyant and expansive.

Further afield the potentially transcultural nature of the Bahá'í teachings was demonstrated by the establishment of the first Bahá'í groups in the United States (1894). 'Abdu'l-Bahá himself emphasized the importance of this development, and later travelled extensively to visit the fledgling Bahá'í groups in both North America and Europe (1911–13). Small Bahá'í groups were also established in Hawaii, Japan and Australia.

Another important development was 'Abdu'l-Bahá's emphasis on the formation of locally elected councils (Spiritual Assemblies) to administer local Bahá'í activities. This made the organizational role of individual local leaders less important. The overall organization of the religion remained strongly centralized, however. Although 'Abdu'l-Bahá himself spent many of his years of leadership in confinement or under the threat of renewed incarceration by the Ottomans, he still continued to direct the widely-scattered activities of the Bahá'í community, both through a massive correspondence and the visits of his more prominent followers.

Of his writings, the most important single works include his 'treatise on civilization' (*Risáli-yi Madaniyyih*, translated as *The Secret of Divine Civilization*, 1875) in which he detailed the religious principles which should order human society; his table talks with one of his western followers (the *Mufávaḍát*, translated as *Some Answered Questions*) in which he responded to questions about Christianity, theology and the nature of man; and his *Will and Testament* in which he designated his successor and established the future organization of the movement. Also important are the several volumes of his talks in the West (see especially *Paris Talks* and *The Promulgation of Universal Peace*) and his letters (of which almost 27,000 items have been collected so far).

Shoghi Effendi (1897–1957)

Shoghi Effendi Rabbani was 'Abdu'l-Bahá's eldest grandson and was appointed to succeed him as 'Guardian of the Cause of God'. During the period of his leadership (1922–57), the Bahá'í 'Administrative Order' was standardized; the Faith's spiritual and administrative world centre was consolidated in the Haifa-'Akká area; a series of increasingly ambitious expansion plans were adopted, whereby Bahá'í groups became established in most of the countries of the world; and a number of Bahá'í Houses of Worship were built.

Although the overall number of Bahá'ís remained small (increasing from perhaps 100,000 to 200,000), there was a significant diversification of membership. Western Bahá'ís in particular assumed an increasing importance in the expansion of the religion and the exposition of its doctrines.

Shoghi Effendi also added significantly to the corpus of Bahá'í literature, and in addition to his own correspondence (at least 17,500 items), he translated several works of Bahá'í scripture and a Bahá'í history, and penned his own review of the events of the first century of the Bábí–Bahá'í movement, *God Passes By* (1944). Of his letters, particular mention should be made of his lengthy *Advent of Divine Justice* (1939), a challenge to Bahá'ís to propagate and live their religion, and the several letters of the *World Order of Bahá'u'lláh* (1929–36), which detail his views on the scope and purpose of the Bahá'í Revelation.

The Universal House of Justice (1963–)

Shoghi Effendi died unexpectedly and without issue in 1957. A group of leading Bahá'ís, the 'Hands of the Cause', exercised a temporary custodianship until 1963, when the Universal House of Justice was elected as the supreme ruling body of the Bahá'í Faith. Under its leadership various new institutions have been developed, ties with the United Nations, begun under Shoghi Effendi, have been greatly strengthened, and increasing concern has been shown with educational and social development issues.

The messages of the Universal House of Justice are regarded as divinely inspired and thus represent yet another element in the corpus of authoritative writings. In addition to its own writings, the House of Justice has established research and archival departments at the Bahá'í World Centre and has subsequently issued a series of compilations of the writings of the previous Bahá'í leaders on various subjects.

The Bahá'í community itself has greatly expanded since 1963, so that there are now perhaps four and a half million Bahá'ís worldwide. This increase in numbers has been concentrated in the Third World and reflects the Bahá'ís' success in adapting their message to a very wide diversity of peoples in Asia, Africa, Latin America, the Caribbean and the Pacific. Some indication of the present-day distribution of the Bahá'í community is provided by Table I. The Table also shows the marked change that has occurred since the early days of Shoghi Effendi's ministry. In 1928, most Bahá'ís lived in the Middle East (71% of all localities), a sizeable minority in the West (24%), and a small number in the Third World (4%). By 1983, however, the Third World was the dominant area (89%), and the West (11%) and the Middle East (1%) comparatively insignificant. Given the greater size of many of the local Iranian Bahá'í communities, these figures considerably understate the relative importance of the Middle East. Even so, it is likely that fewer than one in ten Bahá'ís are now Iranian.

TABLE I
Bahá'í Distribution by Geographical Area, 1928 and 1983.

	Localities where Bahá'ís reside			
	1928		1983	
	no.	%	no.	%
The Islamic Heartland				
Iran	346	59.8	709	0.6
Middle East and North Africa (excl. Iran)	33	5.7	373	0.3
Asiatic Russia	34	5.9	0	—
Subtotal	413	71.3	1082	1.0
The West				
North America	67	11.6	8716	7.7
Europe	65	11.2	2637	2.3
Anglo-Pacific (Australia, New Zealand and Hawaii	9	1.6	545	0.5
Subtotal	141	24.4	11898	10.6
The Bahá'í Third World				
Latin America and the Caribbean	1	0.2	16276	14.4
Africa (excl. the North)	1	0.2	27385	24.3
South and South East Asia	15	2.6	53044	47.0
East Asia	6	1.0	1216	1.1
Oceania	2	0.3	1875	1.7
Subtotal	25	4.3	99796	88.5
Total	579		112776	

Source: P. Smith, *The Babi and Baha'i Religions*. (Cambridge University Press, 1987), pp. 166-9.

Another aspect of the recent period has been the recrudescence of persecution. Although Bahá'ís believe that theirs is an independent world religion, orthodox and traditionalistic Muslims have tended to regard Bahá'í as a pernicious heresy. This has particularly been the case in Iran, where the Bahá'ís have been persecuted since the movement's inception. Bahá'ís have also been accused of being anti-Islamic and of acting as agents of foreign powers, both charges which the Bahá'ís resolutely deny. The situation for Bahá'ís in Iran has markedly worsened since the Islamic Revolution of 1979, and despite a considerable international outcry, almost two hundred Bahá'ís have been executed, and thousands imprisoned or subjected to considerable duress. Elsewhere in the Muslim world the Bahá'í Faith has been banned in several countries, an additional complicating factor being the situation of the Bahá'í World Centre in the territory of the State of Israel (1948).

Together, the periods of leadership of Shoghi Effendi, the Hands of the Cause and the Universal House of Justice have seen a massive transformation in the religion. Whilst retaining the belief in continuing divine guidance, the original succession of individually charismatic leaders has been replaced by the institutions of the Administrative Order. The corpus of Bahá'í sacred writings has been established and the overall system of Bahá'í teachings systematized. The independence of Bahá'í from its parent religion of Shi'i Islam has been proclaimed, and the distinctive religious identity of the Bahá'ís has been emphasized by the growth of Bahá'í communities amongst a wide diversity of non-Muslim peoples and the subsequent internationalization of Bahá'í cultural styles. Certainly it is a mistake to refer to the Bahá'í Faith as if it were still basically an Iranian religion or Shi'i sect. Sociologically (as well as doctrinally), Bahá'í may now best be regarded as an independent world religious movement, or, if one makes due allowance for its relatively small size, as a world religion.

The Significance of Bahá'í History for Bahá'ís

To understand the significance of Bahá'í history for Bahá'ís we need to go beyond this bare historical account. As part of the 'Western' Judeo-Christian-Islamic religious tradition, the successive Bahá'í leaders have interpreted religious history as an account of the acts of God and of the relationship between God and humanity. Given this perspective, Bahá'ís have readily suffused the historical record with metahistorical, 'mythic' significance.

Thus, for Bahá'ís, Bábí and Bahá'í history represent the latest chapters in a divine drama. The evidences of divine power are to be found in the sinlessness of the Báb and Bahá'u'lláh and in the super-human qualities found in the lives of 'Abdu'l-Bahá and Shoghi Effendi. Such lives also serve as moral exemplars. Earlier generations of Bahá'ís (like the Bábís before them) plentifully attributed miracles to their leaders, but in modern Bahá'í the emphasis is more on the general nature of divine intervention. Faced with suffering and difficulties, confronted by tremendous opposition, and lacking many material advantages, the Bahá'í leaders not only endured, but ultimately triumphed. The expansion of the 'Cause of God' was itself further proof of divine power. Despised and persecuted in the land of its birth, Bahá'í had spread to all the corners of the world and had united in its embrace a great diversity of otherwise antagonistic peoples.

The divine drama also portrayed in archetypal form the battle between good and evil. The cause of truth was in every age opposed by the ignorant and the malicious. The birth of a new divine revelation rallied the supporters of truth whilst at the same time it challenged those with established power. Those religious and political leaders who rejected or persecuted the new revelation ultimately received their due reward in the form of divine chastisement. Again, even within the Bahá'í religion, there was a division between those who exemplified the moral quality of faithfulness and that small minority who broke the covenant of succession and rebelled against the successive leaders of the Faith.

These archetypes of good and evil also formed part of a dialectical progression. The acts of external opposition and internal rebellion represented crises in the teleological 'onward march' of the Faith. Each in turn was eventually overcome or was compensated for by new successful achievements.

2

Religious Doctrines

BAHÁ'Í doctrine can be described under two broad headings: the metaphysical or 'religious' doctrines which form the subject of the present chapter, and the social doctrines — the vision of a new society — which are the subject of the next.

All Bahá'í doctrines are primarily rooted in the revelations of Bahá'u'lláh and the supplementary interpretations of 'Abdu'l-Bahá and Shoghi Effendi. All of these are regarded as divinely authoritative. Basically a legislative body, the Universal House of Justice is only incidentally a source of Bahá'í doctrine.

The present chapter is organized around five metaphysical themes: God and creation; divine intermediaries — the 'Manifestations of God'; 'progressive revelation'; human nature and purpose; and suffering the evil. There is also a short final section on the nature of knowledge.

God and Creation

For Bahá'ís, the purpose of human creation is that human beings might know, love and worship God. At the same time, however, God is so transcendent that *'every effort to approach His exalted Self and envisage His Essence hath resulted in hopelessness and failure'*.[1] This paradox lies at the heart of the Bahá'í conception of God and the balance between divine transcendence and imminence.

In essence, God is regarded as utterly transcendent. The universe is God's creation and he is its absolute ruler. All existence is dependent upon him, and from him all beings derive their sustenance. He is independent of all things. He is alone and without equal. No being can know or approach him. He will *'everlastingly continue to be wrapt in the impenetrable mystery of His unknowable Essence'*.[2]

How then can anything be known of God? The Bahá'í answer is that God is known through his attributes and signs, most notably through his love and his command or word. God's love suffuses creation. Veiled in the 'ancient eternity' of his essence, God knew of his love for humankind: 'I loved thy creation, hence I created thee.'[3] This creation was accomplished by the divine command, the word of God (the logos), or, synonymously, the holy spirit or primal will.[4] This realm of God's command is a distinct and separate order of existence. It is the intermediary between the unknowable divine essence and the world of creation. Through the holy spirit, God's will and purpose is manifested to his creatures, and again, through the holy spirit, human beings are enabled to dimly perceive the divine realities.

In the world of creation God's attributes, as revealed by the holy spirit, are variously manifested. At the most general level, each created thing has been made the bearer of some sign of divine reality, so that the whole creation mirrors forth the beauty of God. More specifically, and uniquely, human beings have been made the bearers of all the divine names and attributes. Thus they may be said to have been created in the 'image' of God. They are the lamps in which may be found the divine light, and if they would but turn unto themselves, they would find God standing within them 'mighty, powerful and self-subsisting'.[5] Important as these revelations are, however, they are overshadowed by the chief worldly locus of the divine attributes: the messengers or 'Manifestations' of God.

The Manifestations of God

Bahá'í religious doctrine may be said to centre on the figure of the Manifestation of God. Human beings have been endowed with the capacity to mirror forth all the attributes of God, but even when they attempt to do this they are unable to escape their limitations as part of the world of creation. By contrast, those individuals who have been chosen to be Manifestations of God directly embody the holy spirit. They are the word of God in the world of creation, and through them the divine challenge and summons is addressed to all human beings. They exemplify most perfectly God's attributes and they provide the pure channel for the revelation of God's command. They are both religious exemplars and the revealers of divine law.

The Manifestations of God dwell in the realm of God's command. As such, they are a distinct reality and are *in essence* neither God nor human beings. However, they make their physical appearance in the human world and by so doing take on a two-fold station: human and divine. Thus, in terms of their humanity, they are subject to all the normal human realities of birth and death, physical suffering, emotional experience and family relationships. At the same time, in terms of their divine station, they represent the Godhead to humanity, and as such, speak with the 'voice' of God. Indeed, in their divine station, they may claim divinity in relationship to ordinary human beings. This two-fold station is reflected in the diversity of religious claims which the Manifestations make for themselves.

There is no definitive listing of Manifestations in the Bahá'í writings. Explicitly included are the major figures of the Western Asian religious tradition: Abraham, Moses, Jesus Christ and Muḥammad. To these are added Zoroaster, Gautama Buddha, the Báb and Bahá'u'lláh. Adam is also included, not as first man as in the biblical account, but as the first recorded Manifestation of God in human development, there being others who are unknown who preceded him. Most Bahá'ís also add the Hindu figure of Krishna to the list of Manifestations. Regardless of the exact listing, the general principle is clear, however: As long as humanity has existed as a separate species, God has periodically sent his messengers to guide all human beings to the path of truth. Similarly, this provision of guidance will be extended into the future for as long as humanity continues to exist. Various other figures of religious history are explicitly excluded from the list of Manifestations and are instead regarded as moral reformers and sages (Confucius) or as minor prophets who are divinely inspired but not the bearers of an independent divine revelation (the prophets of Israel). Nevertheless, these minor prophets and reformers contribute to the spiritual renewal of humanity.

Progressive Revelation

Bahá'ís believe that the provision of divine guidance expresses a single 'plan of God'. All the Manifestations of God come from the same source and proclaim aspects of a single divine religion. From this standpoint many of the divisions between the various world religions are essentially man-made and are the consequence of fallible human beings attempting to systematize and delimit the boundless ocean of divine revelation.

However, the Bahá'ís do not believe that there are no differences between the teachings of the various Manifestations. Each expresses the eternal truths of God, but each also addresses a more specific message to the particular people amongst whom he appears. Given the diversity of social and historical contexts, these specific messages necessarily differ. Each is suited to the religious and social needs of a particular age. Again, differences also result from the fact that each Manifestation of God is born into a particular human culture and that consequently his words are expressed in the distinctive language and conceptual frameworks of that culture.

Bahá'ís refer to the overall pattern of divine guidance as a process of 'progressive revelation'. Human history and society are seen as evolutionary in nature. Whilst subject to regular periods of retrogression, the human capacity for spiritual and social development is regarded as having increased over time. The successive Manifestations of God have accordingly revealed an ever greater measure of divine guidance appropriate to the evolutionary stages of human development. The process of social development, which earlier saw the emergence of tribes, city-states and nations, is now close to its culmination in the creation of a single world society: the social stage for which Bahá'u'lláh's teachings are specifically geared. Future Manifestations of God will consolidate and extend God's spiritual and social teachings for this new world society.

Progressive revelation is punctuated into a series of 'dispensations', each marking the allotted period for the dominance of the teachings of a particular Manifestation of God. (Thus in Western Asia, the successive dispensations are those of Abraham, Moses, Jesus, Muḥammad, the Báb and Bahá'u'lláh.) Each Manifestation appears at a time of spiritual trial, delivers the revelation of which he is the bearer, and thereby initiates a cycle of spiritual renewal.

In the course of time, his teachings become crystallized into a religious system which provides the basis for a new religious civilization. Given the limitations of the human spirit, this crystallization ultimately leads to spiritual stagnation and the attempt to revive the original freshness and purity of the religion. When these attempts at renewal have finally failed, a new Manifestation of God appears, often to the accompaniment of the vehement opposition of the institutional leaders of the previous religious establishment.

Human Nature and Purpose

Human beings have both a spiritual and a physical nature. Spiritually, they are empowered to reflect the attributes of God. Physically, they are constrained by their sensual emotions and lusts such as anger, jealousy, disputatiousness, covetousness, avarice, hate, cruelty, pride and the desire to dominate. Human beings derive these sensual qualities from their animal existence, but what may be 'natural' in animals is unnatural and sinful in human beings. Humans share an animal existence, but they also transcend it with their intellectual and spiritual potentialities, the ability consciously to know and worship God sharply differentiating humans from other animals.

Given this distinction, the primary purpose of human life is to realize spiritual potential and to struggle to control the sensual qualities of human animality. This process of transformation stems in the first instance from the guidance and sustaining love of the holy spirit, particularly as revealed by the Manifestations of God. It is sustained by the human endeavour to remain faithful to the spirit and teachings of the divine messengers, and by the development of the power of conscience.

The process of transformation occurs at both an individual and collective level. Individually, it focuses on the human soul. Bahá'ís believe that each individual human being possesses an inner spiritual reality or soul. This soul comes into being at the moment of conception, and continues to exist in various spiritual realms after the dissolution of the physical body. It does not return to the physical world in any sense of reincarnation. During the individual's life in this world he or she attains a greater or lesser degree of spiritual and moral development. By so doing, the individual largely determines his or her state of soul in the spiritual realms of the afterlife. As there is no limit to the degree of spiritual development, there is no simple division between those who are saved and those who are not (heaven and hell are regarded as states of soul rather than actual locations, 'heaven' representing nearness to God and 'hell' separation from him). The detailed nature of the afterlife is regarded as beyond the ability of those who are still alive in the present world to comprehend.

Human transformation also occurs at a collective level, and one of the purposes of human creation is for humanity as a whole to draw nearer to God. Individual salvation, therefore, cannot be separated from the more general concern to work to foster an 'ever-advancing civilization'. True spirituality does not consist of a monastic withdrawal from the concerns of the world, but of a religious commitment to transforming the world in the light of divine teachings. The Bahá'í social teachings, outlined in the next chapter, do not represent merely a programme of social reform, but are intended to serve as the guidelines for the fundamental spiritual transformation of the human race.

Suffering and Evil

Suffering is endemic to the human condition. Bahá'ís acknowledge this reality and simultaneously seek both to accept and work against it. Thus, on the one hand, Bahá'ís are not fatalists and are encouraged to work actively to mitigate the causes of human suffering and to avoid such actions as may cause harm to themselves or to others. At the same time, however, they are taught to regard suffering as a potential cause of spiritual development, a divine test leading the individual to greater resolve and to detachment from this transitory world.

In accounting for suffering, Bahá'ís only make incidental appeal to the notion of evil. Indeed, Bahá'ís believe that evil has no positive existence as an independent metaphysical force (such as a devil). Individual human beings commit evil or selfish actions, but they do so because of their own spiritual weaknesses.

Their temptation comes from their own baser instincts and not from an external satan. Unless mentally incapable, they exercise free will and are responsible for their own moral decisions. Terms such as 'satan' are purely symbolic of these baser instincts.

Knowledge

All religions assume particular theories of knowledge. According to the Bahá'í view, there is no essential division between different forms of knowledge. All true knowledge is ultimately of God or his creation. Access to this knowledge may be obtained from various sources. Divine revelation through the Manifestations of God is of central importance, but knowledge can also be obtained through the individual's own inspiration and contemplation of reality. This conception leads Bahá'ís to emphasize the value of both contemplation and scientific rationality as well as religious tradition. From this standpoint, science and religion are simply two expressions of one reality. They are complementary bases for human knowledge.

There is no limit to the extent to which human beings can gain knowledge. But at the same time, all human knowledge is inherently fallible. Human sense perceptions, reasoning and inspiration are all fallible, but so also is human knowledge based on religious tradition and authority as this is mediated through human understanding. This would appear to imply that all knowledge is provisional in nature. The best that can be done is to check one source of knowledge against another. The complementarity of science and religion thus assumes particular importance. In general, both should rest upon *the premises and conclusions of reason* and should *bear its test*.[6] More specifically, science and reason provide a means of differentiating between true religion and mere superstition, whilst divine revelation provides a standard by which scientific statements and theories can be judged. Divine revelation also represents a potential source of scientific knowledge.

The Bahá'í attitude towards knowledge has important implications for the individual's own relationship to religion. Throughout Bahá'í history there has been a continuing emphasis on the authority of the successive leaders of the Bahá'í Faith, but this emphasis must be placed alongside an insistence on the importance of the individual's own independent investigation of truth and on the right of individual self-expression. There appears to be an implicit tension here.

3

Social Doctrines

CENTRAL to the Bahá'í religion is a vision of a new world order. Bahá'u'lláh is regarded by Bahá'ís as the prophesied redeemer of all the religions of the past. He has come therefore to establish the 'kingdom of God' on earth. For Bahá'ís, this kingdom, the 'Most Great Peace', represents the supreme objective of human collective endeavour. In it there will be complete world unity and peace. Society will be grounded on moral and religious principles. And the resources of the world and its peoples will be directed towards whatever secures the advancement and betterment of humankind.

This kingdom will not appear mysteriously. It will be established as the consequence of a lengthy period of preparation in which humanity will become unified and spiritualized. To work for the unification and spiritualization of the human race is thus the most urgent task facing the people of the contemporary world.

This millennial vision is the goal of Bahá'í activity, but Bahá'ís see themselves as the leaven rather than as the sole promoters of the necessary processes of transformation. All men and women of goodwill can contribute to the task of making the world a better world. More forcefully, human society is itself subject to a variety of economic, political and cultural processes which increasingly impel a reluctant humanity towards world unity. The existing world order simply no longer works and will have to change.

The Bahá'í vision may be described as pragmatically idealistic. That is, whilst concerned to portray their own vision of the future, the successive leaders of the Bahá'í Faith have shown a willingness to begin with mundane realities and to try to work constructively from that base. From this standpoint, their message is directed to all people and not just to Bahá'ís.

International Order

This pragmatic attitude is evidenced by Bahá'u'lláh's distinction between the 'Most Great Peace' – the promised kingdom of God on earth – and the 'Lesser Peace', a more limited peace between the nations. The accomplishment of this 'Lesser Peace' formed an important theme in Bahá'u'lláh's letters to the rulers (1860s–70s); in 'Abdu'l-Bahá's public addresses in the West (1911–13); in Bahá'í support for the work of the United Nations (1947–); and most recently in the Universal House of Justice's message 'to the peoples of the world', *The Promise of World Peace* (1985).

For the Bahá'ís, peace among the nations is an achievable and essential goal of the present century. Its achievement depends upon the implementation of the principles of collective security, by which an all-embracing assembly of the world's rulers should establish a universal and binding peace treaty guaranteeing the territorial integrity of each nation and delimiting its military forces. Subsequent differences should be resolved by an international court of arbitration, or *in extremis* by collective intervention against any aggressor nation. A body such as the United Nations (but with greater powers than the present UN) would provide a satisfactory base for the implementation of these principles, whilst the increasing costs of armaments will eventually provide a major economic incentive towards their adoption.

More generally, the independent work of individuals, organizations and governments can be influential. In a climate of international bellicosity and despair, a fundamental change in human values needs to be promoted. The uncritical acceptance of the belief that human beings are irredeemably violent needs to be challenged, and each individual needs to engage in the struggle against his or her own prejudices and feelings of aggression. The full political emancipation of women will greatly enhance the move towards greater peacefulness.

The Oneness of Humanity

The Bahá'ís view the achievement of a lasting international peace as being closely linked to work towards a number of other objectives. Central here is the general recognition of the oneness and unity of the human race. Much human animosity is fuelled by the concern with the differences between peoples of different races, religions, nations and classes. These animosities are sustained by numerous prejudices, and the feelings of both prejudice and animosity need to be replaced by a consciousness of human unity. God has created all human beings as '*the leaves of one tree and the drops of one ocean*', and the time has now come for all people to acknowledge that their unity as human beings transcends their social and cultural differences.[7] Any means that increases the sense of human solidarity is to be welcomed. Thus, for example, Bahá'ís advocate the adoption of an international language to be taught as a single auxiliary language to all the world's peoples.

The growth of human solidarity must entail the ending of all forms of institutionalized racism and the erosion of prejudices. In the case of oppressed minority groups, some positive discrimination may be necessary, that is, steps should be taken to ensure that depressed groups are able to achieve their basic educational and social rights. But otherwise, all forms of discriminatory practice need to be abolished. More generally, it is necessary to work for reconciliation between the various nationalities, races and religions. In this task, loving-kindness, wisdom, and careful consultation are necessary. Consultation must include a recognition that long-lasting patterns of discrimination are corruptive of both victims and oppressors, and that the resultant feelings of suspicion and superiority are an integral part of the problem.

With regard to nationalist sentiment, it is necessary to recognize that unrestricted state sovereignty is simply no longer possible in the modern world. The major problems that face mankind are global in nature, and economic or political isolationism is not a viable option. International interdependence is now a paramount reality, and feelings of human solidarity should reflect this. This does not mean that national or separate cultural identities should be disparaged. Rather, human diversity is to be welcomed as long as it does not threaten the overarching unity of the human race.

As to religious divisions, these should not constitute a basis for social strife. Such strife not only often contradicts the spirit of the teachings of the various religions, but impedes the development of human understanding and spiritual values. Religionists should work with the followers of other faiths to promote human fellowship and amity.

Economic Justice

Whilst teaching the need for individuals to be detached from material desires and possessions, the successive Bahá'í leaders emphasized the importance of the economic base for the development of a just and spiritual society. As 'Abdu'l-Bahá observed, the struggle for physical survival represents *'the fountain-head of all calamities'*, lack of basic material means being a form of enslavement which degrades and demoralizes human beings.[8]

To create a just society, all forms of economic and chattel slavery need to be abolished. Individuals need to have legally-established rights to an adequate basic wage and pension. Those who are unable to provide for themselves need to receive the basic necessities of life. These objectives can be achieved both by government intervention and voluntary endeavour on the part of the rich. Absolute equality will always be unachievable, but the extremes of wealth and poverty need to be abolished (by such means as progressive taxation). Again, businesses should establish profit-sharing schemes with their workers, and the wealthy should become more conscious of their social and moral obligations towards the poor. Certainly, by denying these obligations, the rich jeopardize their own spiritual futures and contribute directly to social unrest.

Political Order

The Bahá'í teachings on political order emphasize the need for both stability and justice. For Bahá'u'lláh and his successors, political stability is essential, for without it, society itself is threatened by anarchy and chaos. Some constraint on human behaviour is necessary: unlimited freedom brings with it the danger of sedition and depravity. Human dignity and liberty are best served by submission to the laws of God, but as the fear of God is not an innate human characteristic, it is necessary for governments to impose their own systems of order. It is a religious duty to be loyal to such governments, even when their ordinances are imperfect.

This emphasis on the essential need for order is accompanied by an appeal for justice and for respect for individual freedom. Injustice and arbitrary rule are condemned, most importantly on moral grounds, but also because they destroy social solidarity and weaken nations. In a just and effective government, the exercise of power is constrained by the bounds of constitutional legality, by the institution of consultative political structures, and by the establishment of due processes of law which recognize the equal rights of all. Again, the separation of powers, as between a legislature and a judiciary, and federal rather than extremely centralized forms of government, represent defences against despotism.

More than this is needed, however. Democratic government by itself is not a sure defence against corruption and injustice. Both electors and elected need to be educated so that they can understand the issues of the day and the moral imperatives of democracy. Indeed, an uneducated populace may long for justice, but if they lack 'even the vocabulary to explain what they want', then they will continue to be oppressed.[9] Again, every individual needs to be able to enjoy freedom of speech and conscience, to have access to a free and responsible press, and to be unhindered in his or her participation in the processes of election and consultation.

Sexual Equality

According to the Bahá'í teachings, one of the major barriers to human unity and advancement is the prevailing inequality between the sexes. Men and women are created equally in the image of God and they are equal in their potentialities of

LAKEWOOD MEMORIAL LIBRARY
LAKEWOOD, NEW YORK 14750

intelligence, virtue and prowess. That women are so commonly prevented from attaining their full potential is the result of their lack of education and their oppression by men. Both of these contexts must change.

At a legal and institutional level, women must attain full legal, political and educational equality with men. At the same time, women must strive to advance in all areas of human life and increase in confidence. For their part, men must abandon their historic prejudices and realize that human advancement as a whole can only occur when both sexes are involved as equal partners.

Universal Education

The Bahá'í vision of a new world order depends upon a number of important institutional changes, but underlying changes of attitude seem generally to be given even more importance. In effecting such changes, great emphasis is placed on education, secular, moral and religious.

Every individual should have the right to basic education, including instruction in reading and writing, and the acquisition of the skills necessary to conduct a trade or profession. Beyond this, education is seen as a potential means of promoting the sense of human solidarity and equality, tolerance, respect for justice and order, political responsibility and the desire for human advancement.

Education is not confined to the classroom. A commitment to education should become a general concern of society. Parents, and in particular mothers, have a basic educational responsibility before and beyond anything provided by the school. In cases of limited resources, girls, as potential mothers of the future, and as such their children's first teachers, should have educational priority.

Spiritual and Material Civilization

For Bahá'ís, these various social principles represent vital elements in the building of the kingdom of God on earth. They form part of a wider vision and are not simply necessary social reforms. Bahá'ís may advocate social change and concern themselves with aspects of 'material' development, but they do not believe that these of themselves are sufficient. For a true world civilization to develop, material and spiritual elements need to be combined. Only by the spiritual transformation of human beings can life be filled with moral purpose, and it is only through that transformation that high ideals can be changed into practical objectives.

4

Morality and Spirituality

BECOMING a Bahá'í should entail a spiritual transformation. It is not enough simply to call oneself by a particular religious label: '*a man may call himself a Bahá'í for fifty years, [but] if he does not live the life he is not a Bahá'í.*'[10]

To 'live the life' requires love, faith and deeds. Love is essentially the relationship between the individual soul and God. God's love is his stronghold, '*he that entereth therein is safe and secure, and he that turneth away shall surely stray and perish*'.[11] Enriched by God's love, the individual is enabled to realize the virtues which lie latent within his or her own self. Made alive by God's bounty, the individual can begin the process of transformation by which his relationship with God becomes closer and his earthly life is transformed.

Tied to love are faith and the knowledge of God. By trusting in God, we increase our reliance on him and we lessen our reliance on our own limited capacities. By this means, we are able to increase our detachment from the material world and not to sorrow at its tests and difficulties. Again, by trusting in God we become more conscious of God's will and purpose, and are enabled to transcend our own limitations by attuning ourselves to God's will and to the dynamic force of the holy spirit. Similarly, by knowing God – or rather, God's attributes as revealed by the Manifestations of God and as evidenced in creation and in our own selves – we increase our faith and knowledge of his purpose.

Deeds are the third vital element in living the life. Faith is evidenced in deeds. Deeds here include moral and philanthropic actions, the development of a general attitude of detachment from

the world and obedience to the ordinances revealed by the
Manifestations of God.

Individual Morality

Bahá'u'lláh has written that *'the light of a good character surpasseth
the light of the sun'*.[12] Some impression of the Bahá'í conception of
good character may be gained from the following passage:

> *Be generous in prosperity, and thankful in adversity.*
> *Be worthy of the trust of thy neighbour, and look upon him with a bright and
> friendly face.*
> *Be a treasure to the poor, an admonisher to the rich, an answerer of the cry of
> the needy, a preserver of the sanctity of thy pledge.*
> *Be fair in thy judgement, and guarded in thy speech.*
> *Be unjust to no man, and show all meekness to all men.*
> *Be as a lamp unto them that walk in darkness, a joy to the sorrowful, a sea
> for the thirsty, a haven for the distressed,*
> *an upholder and defender of the victim of oppression.*
> *Let integrity and uprightness distinguish all thine acts.*
> *Be a home for the stranger, a balm to the suffering, a tower of strength for the
> fugitive.*
> *Be eyes to the blind, and a guiding light unto the feet of the erring.*
> *Be an ornament to the countenance of truth,*
> *a crown to the brow of fidelity,*
> *a pillar of the temple of righteousness,*
> *a breath of life to the body of mankind,*
> *an ensign of the hosts of justice,*
> *a luminary above the horizon of virtue,*
> *a dew to the soil of the human heart,*
> *an ark on the ocean of knowledge,*
> *a sun in the heaven of bounty,*
> *a gem on the diadem of wisdom,*
> *a shining light in the firmament of thy generation,*
> *a fruit upon the tree of humility.*[13]

The moral ideals of the Bahá'í Faith may be described in more
detail in terms of six general themes: justice, trustworthiness,
moral purity, fraternity, respect and kindness. Of these, justice
and equity are the most fundamental human virtues, the *'best*

beloved of all things' in God's sight.[14] As individual qualities, they demand vigilance against being unjust towards others and consideration of the rights of all those involved in a particular situation. Again, the exercise of fairness requires that the individual should only desire for others what he desires for himself. This undeviating sense of individual justice, however, is not to be confused with the exercise of any moralistic judgementalism, as judgement is regarded as a societal rather than individual concern: as individuals, we should not judge each other lest we ourselves be judged. Thus, the individual should show forbearance, forgiveness and love towards others, should not *'breathe the sins'* of others or despise the sinful, and should remember his own faults and shortcomings rather than those of others.

Next to justice and equity, trustworthiness and truthfulness are particularly praised in the Bahá'í writings. Thus 'Abdu'l-Bahá refers to truthfulness as being the foundation of other virtues without which the soul's progress and success are impossible. Similarly, he refers to lying as the most blameworthy quality, *'the destroyer of all human perfections, and the cause of innumerable vices'*.[15] As for trustworthiness, Bahá'u'lláh describes it as an essential condition for the stability and security of human life.

The third theme which can be identified is that of moral purity. God has chosen the human 'heart' to be the *'seat for the revelation of His glory'*, and the heart should therefore be sanctified from every worldly defilement.[16] By this token, Bahá'ís should endeavour to lead a chaste and holy life. They should be modest, decent, temperate and clean-minded. They should exercise moderation in dress, language, amusements and artistic avocations. They should exercise constant control of their carnal desires and corrupt inclinations. They should avoid frivolity. They should absolutely abstain from the use of alcohol and habit-forming drugs, and from easy sexual familiarity and sexual vice. At the same time, however, they should avoid becoming puritanical bigots or ascetics. The world's pleasures are bestowed by God, and as long as one's motives are pure, and one abstains from what is forbidden by God, then life is to be enjoyed.[17] For example, Bahá'ís have no objection to music, dancing or public entertainments as long as these pursuits are conducted with moral rectitude; and their homes should be havens of peace, joy and laughter.

The fourth theme is fraternity. All human beings are the children of one God. As such, all merit love and kindness. Thus, 'Abdu'l-Bahá enjoins his 'friends' to consort with the peoples of the world with '*the utmost truthfulness, uprightness, faithfulness, kindliness, good-will and friendliness*', and to seek to dispel ignorance, enmity, hate, rancour and estrangement.[18] Such kindness must not be limited by any division of religion, nationality or race. Any prejudices or feelings of superiority based on such differences must be abandoned.

The fifth theme is that of dignity and respect. Human beings are endowed with divine virtue. For this reason, each individual should respect the divine creation that is a human being. This includes respect for his or her own self, not only in terms of seeking to realize spiritual perfections and abandoning selfish desires but also by becoming '*the essence of cleanliness among mankind*', and by being refined and dignified in manner and dress.[19] Again, even though it is only a physical quality, cleanliness exercises a positive influence on spirituality.

As to respect for others, this requires courtesy, tact, patience, wisdom and a sin-covering eye. Each person should avoid becoming a source of grief or despondency to others. Again, each person should look for the good qualities of others rather than the bad, and on no account should anyone detract or slander others. Indeed, back-biting is regarded as a most grievous sin and one which is cursed by God.[20]

The final theme is that of loving-kindness towards others. If we love God, then we will see our fellow human beings as our brothers and sisters, and show them kindness and goodwill. Indeed, we should prefer others to ourselves. Kindness to animals is also enjoined.

Detachment

Spiritual development requires more than the endeavour to realize a set of moral injunctions. The Bahá'í teachings encourage an attitude of general detachment from material concerns, but at the same time prohibit extreme asceticism or seclusion from the world. Bahá'ís are bidden to live in the world but not to become worldly. They should seek to acquire spiritual qualities in the midst of everyday life and in service to their fellow human beings. They should allow nothing to come between themselves and God.

The Laws of God: Acts of Devotion

For Bahá'ís, 'good deeds' include obedience to the laws of God revealed by Bahá'u'lláh as the Manifestation of God. These include a number of specific ordinances which relate to individual spiritual transformation. Many of these 'acts of devotion' form part of the corpus of Bahá'í religious law, and as such are regarded as binding upon Bahá'í practice. Unlike the communal laws of the Bahá'í Faith discussed in the next chapter, the enforcement of these spiritual ordinances is left to the individual conscience. Four such ordinances will here be considered: prayer, fasting, giving to the Bahá'í Fund and teaching.

Prayer

Prayer and meditation are vital elements in the development of a Bahá'í way of life. Central to the purpose of prayer is that it forms a connection between the individual and God. By turning to God and seeking God's love and compassion the individual turns away from material attachments and increases his spiritual perception. In this state he becomes more open to divine guidance. It is necessary to strive to attain this state, but even the mere act of prayer will ultimately have an effect on the individual's soul. Prayer for Bahá'ís is therefore an obligatory act as well as an element in the individual's own spiritual quest.

The obligatory aspect of Bahá'í prayer centres on the daily use of one of three special prayers revealed by Bahá'u'lláh. These 'obligatory prayers' are of varying lengths and complexity, and the individual has the choice of which to use each day. The shortest of the three prayers is worded as follows:

I bear witness, O my God, that Thou hast created me to know Thee and to worship Thee. I testify, at this moment, to my powerlessness and to Thy might, to my poverty and to Thy wealth.

There is none other God but Thee, the Help in Peril, the Self-Subsisting. [21]

In Islamic fashion, in their full form, all three prayers are preceded by simple ritual ablutions (washing of the hands and face). The two longer prayers are also accompanied by prostrations and gestures of supplication towards God, and there are set times at which two of the prayers should be said. Unlike the Islamic ritual prayer, the Bahá'í obligatory prayers are always said privately (usually in the home) and not congregationally.

In addition to the obligatory prayers, Bahá'ís are bidden to chant or read the Bahá'í scriptures every morning and evening, and to bring themselves to account each day, before '*death, unheralded, shall come upon thee and thou shalt be called to give account for thy deeds*'. [22] The actual details of these observances are left to the individual.

As to private prayer and meditation, Bahá'ís are encouraged to use the prayers of the Bahá'í leaders (Bahá'u'lláh, 'Abdu'l-Bahá, Shoghi Effendi) and of the Báb. There are hundreds of these 'supplications', and they represent a variety of concerns: requests for divine aid and assistance in the attainment of spiritual qualities, or in teaching the Bahá'í Faith, or in service to humanity; prayers of gratitude to God; prayers for protection from tests, for unity, for healing, for the upbringing of children, for guidance and for forgiveness; and prayers for use at dawn or in the 'dark night'. Many of these prayers conclude with a listing of some of God's attributes, as in this prayer of 'Abdu'l-Bahá:

O Thou compassionate Lord, Thou Who art generous and able! We are servants of Thine sheltered beneath Thy providence. Cast Thy glance of favour upon us. Give light to our eyes, hearing to our ears, and understanding and love to our hearts. Render our souls joyous and happy through Thy glad tidings. O Lord! Point out to us the pathway of Thy kingdom and resuscitate all of us through the breaths of the Holy Spirit. Bestow upon us life everlasting and confer upon us never-ending honour. Unify mankind and illumine the world of humanity. May we all follow Thy pathway, long for Thy good pleasure and seek the mysteries of Thy kingdom. O God! Unite us and connect our hearts with Thy indissoluble bond. Verily, Thou art the Giver, Thou art the Kind One and Thou art the Almighty.[23]

There are also a number of prayers which are regarded as having a special potency, such as the 'Long Healing Prayer', or the Tablet of Aḥmad, which was particularly revealed for those 'in affliction or grief'.

Private prayer is linked to meditation. Meditation is regarded as a subjective state in which the individual withdraws himself from consciousness of external objects and employs his inward power of vision. If in this state the individual is turned towards God, then he may become *'immersed in the ocean of spiritual life'*. However, if the individual is not turned towards God, then the inspiration derived from his meditation will simply reflect his own ego. For this reason, Bahá'ís are particularly encouraged to meditate on the Bahá'í writings: to immerse themselves in the ocean of God's words, so that they may *'unravel its secrets, and discover all the pearls of wisdom that lie hid in its depths'*.[24] No set meditational techniques are outlined, however, and the form of meditation is regarded as a matter of personal choice. Shoghi Effendi has outlined five steps of prayer which link prayer and meditation to decision-making and action, but these are regarded only as personal suggestions rather than as an authoritative statement.[25] More generally, Bahá'ís are advised that if they do adopt particular forms of prayer or meditation, they should avoid superstitious practices or the introduction of divisive rituals and customs. Bahá'ís are also advised not to become proud as a result of excessive devotions. Again, the purpose of prayer (and meditation) is to refresh the soul and not to exhaust it, thus *'to chant but one verse with joy and gladness'* is better than *'reading all the Revelations of the Omnipotent God with carelessness'*.[26]

As well as individual prayer, Bahá'ís also meet together to pray, and most Bahá'í meetings will begin and end with prayers. Invariably these are the written prayers of the Bahá'í leaders. These include prayers for particular occasions such as holy day commemorations, weddings and funerals.

Fasting

Fasting augments the spiritual exercise of prayer. The Bahá'í fast consists of complete abstention from food and drink between the hours of sunrise and sunset for the nineteen days of the Bahá'í month of 'Alá (Loftiness; 2–20 March). All adult Bahá'ís (aged 15–70) are under a spiritual obligation to fast unless they are pregnant, nursing mothers, sick, travelling, or in some other way prevented from fulfilling their obligation.

The act of abstinence is itself only symbolic. The essential purpose of the fast is that it should be a period of spiritual renewal, in which the believer should pray and meditate, refresh and reinvigorate the spiritual forces latent in his soul, and strive to readjust his inner life by ridding himself of selfish and carnal desires. The fast also serves to remind the believer of the detachment of the Manifestations of God.

Donations to the Bahá'í Fund

Bahá'ís regard generosity as a divine attribute and are encouraged to emulate it. Such generosity may well include acts of charity, but the primary emphasis in the Bahá'í writings is on generosity in support of the Bahá'í Fund, that is the various sums of money used to accomplish the objectives of the Bahá'í Faith and its administrative order (see Chapter 6). Giving to the Bahá'í Fund is a voluntary act and is made in secret. Only Bahá'ís may give to the Fund. Such giving is regarded as a prime spiritual responsibility. All Bahá'ís are encouraged to sacrifice their own wants and desires in order to support the Fund, and regard such support as a means of judging the degree of their own faith and devotion to the Bahá'í Cause and as a means of attracting divine assistance. Spiritually, it is the degree of sacrifice, and not the amount that is given, which is important. Rich and poor should both be able to feel a sense of participation. However, whilst learning the spiritual principle of reliance on God, the individual should not incur debts in order to give to the Fund. Nor should he forget his other financial obligations.

In addition to these voluntary contributions, Bahá'u'lláh

instituted a special fund called the *ḥuqúqu'lláh* (the right of God). This consists of a 'tax' assessment of nineteen percent on the positive balance of a year's income over essential expenditure. This payment is a spiritual obligation akin to obligatory prayer and fasting, but at present it is not levied universally throughout the Bahá'í world.

Teaching and Service

For Bahá'ís, the Cause and teachings of Bahá'u'lláh are the 'sovereign remedy' for all the world's problems. They themselves are a leaven in the divine plan for humankind. As such, they have a supreme obligation to work to promote the Bahá'í Cause, not only by teaching about the Bahá'í Faith to others — in itself a sacred responsibility — but also by seeking to perfect their characters as individuals, by working to develop and mature the Bahá'í Administrative Order, and by assisting in the establishment of a tightly-knit worldwide Bahá'í community.

More generally, Bahá'ís should work for the service of humankind and regard work itself — particularly when performed in the spirit of service to others — as being a form of worship to God.

5

Community Life

EVERY religious movement has its own pattern of community life defined by such criteria as its conception of membership, its regulation of social life, and the form and nature of its communal gatherings.

Membership

In the case of the Bahá'í Faith, great stress is placed on the voluntary nature of membership, and commitment is regarded as the consequence of an individual's search after truth. The decision to become a Bahá'í is then basically an individual decision which most Bahá'í Assemblies readily ratify. (For a discussion of Bahá'í Spiritual Assemblies and other elements of Bahá'í administration, see Chapter 6.) There are no formal requirements of membership apart from acceptance by the appropriate Bahá'í Assembly, and only in the most extreme cases is an individual's membership of the Bahá'í community questioned. Consequently, there is a wide range of commitment within the community and an acceptance that individuals will find their own level of involvement.

Membership of the community is open to men, women and children of any racial, religious or social background. There are no gradations of membership other than those of age. In this regard fifteen is regarded as the age of 'legal' maturity, and before this age children are not bound by the requirements of Bahá'í law (e.g. they need not fast and they cannot marry). In turn, 'administrative' majority is attained at the age of twenty-one, Bahá'í youth then gaining their right to vote in Bahá'í elections.

Expulsion from the community only occurs in the case of those

who publicly attack the official line of succession (Bahá'u'lláh–
'Abdu'l-Bahá–Shoghi Effendi–Universal House of Justice) or who
commit a major breach of Bahá'í communal law (for example, by
the non-observance of the Bahá'í marriage laws or persistent
immorality). The former case ('Covenant-breaking') is regarded as
far more serious and amounts to formal excommunication. It is
very rare. The latter case, which leads to a loss of the right to vote
in Bahá'í elections, is more common, although Bahá'í Assemblies
are generally very reluctant to resort to this measure, preferring to
persuade the individual to change his or her ways. At present,
only Bahá'í National Spiritual Assemblies have the right to
remove an individual's voting rights, and appeal against such a
decision may be made to the Universal House of Justice. The
formal excommunication of an individual can only be declared by
the Hands of the Cause and is ratified by the Universal House of
Justice.

The Regulation of Social Life

Religions vary greatly in the extent to which their leaders seek to
advise or to exercise control over the social lives of their
adherents. In the modern Bahá'í community, those areas of life
which are most subject to regulation are marriage; divorce; death
and burial; certain aspects of life-style; and membership of non-
Bahá'í organizations. Other areas of life are comparatively
unregulated; and it is notable that, apart from marriage and
burial, there is no formal commemoration of the main passages of
life (birth and the attainment of religious and legal maturity), nor
is entry into the Bahá'í community normally marked by any
special ceremony.

Regulation takes the form of both general moral counsel and
specific Bahá'í laws. In this latter regard, Bahá'í, like Judaism
and Islam, has a strong conception of the importance of divinely
revealed law, and obedience to God's commands is regarded as an
essential element in the conduct of religious life. Obedience to
much of Bahá'í law (for example, that concerning prayer and
fasting) is regarded as a matter of individual conscience, but in
the main areas of social life, administrative sanctions may be

applied to those who persistently or seriously breach the appropriate ordinances.

For the most part, Bahá'í law derives from the writings of Bahá'u'lláh, but the interpretations of 'Abdu'l-Bahá and Shoghi Effendi together with the supplementary legislation of the Universal House of Justice also constitute a primary source of Bahá'í law.

Marriage, Divorce and Family Life

Bahá'ís place great stress on the importance of marriage and a stable family life. Marriage is encouraged, and in its ideal state is regarded as a spiritual relationship which will endure throughout 'the worlds of God'. That is, true marriage does not end with death. For this reason, Bahá'ís are advised to choose as a marriage partner someone who will be a true companion and comrade. Marriage is monogamous, and concubinage and polygamy are forbidden, as are any sexual relationships outside of marriage. Sex is regarded as a normal part of human life, but it may only be legitimately expressed within the marriage relationship. Divorce is permitted but is strongly discouraged.

Bahá'ís may be engaged or marry from the age of fifteen upwards. All Bahá'í marriages require the consent of the bride and groom, and also of all their living parents. This latter stipulation is made in order to strengthen the ties of duty between parents and children. The Bahá'í marriage ceremony takes place under the aegis of a Bahá'í Spiritual Assembly. All that is generally required is that the bride and groom each repeat the verse *'We will all, verily, abide by the Will of God'* in front of two witnesses, and that the Assembly is satisfied that consent has been given to the marriage by the bridal pair and their parents. Beyond this basic minimum, there are no ceremonial requirements, the bridal pair generally specifying the details of their own ceremony. This will commonly include the reading of various Bahá'í prayers and writings on marriage, but there is no set form, and celebrations will often reflect local cultural patterns. Simplicity is encouraged. Middle Eastern Bahá'ís are subject to two additional requirements: an engagement period prior to marriage of no more than ninety-five days, and the payment of a small dowry by the husband to the wife. As with other aspects of Bahá'í law, these requirements will eventually be extended to all Bahá'ís.

Marriage to non-Bahá'ís is allowed, but a Bahá'í marriage ceremony must take place. The Bahá'í partner can also take part in the marriage ceremony of the religion of the non-Bahá'í spouse, as long as by so doing his or her faith is not compromised. It is also possible for two non-Bahá'ís to be married according to Bahá'í law under the aegis of the Spiritual Assembly.

Whilst upholding the ideal of Bahá'í marriage, Bahá'ís recognize that marriages do break down and that divorce may become necessary. As divorce is strongly deprecated, it is the duty of a Bahá'í Spiritual Assembly to seek to reconcile a husband and wife whose marriage is in jeopardy. Only if this attempt at reconciliation is unsuccessful can a Bahá'í divorce proceed. Normally the Assembly sets the couple a 'year of patience' during which they must live apart and spiritually reconsider their position. If at the end of the year of patience they are still not reconciled, then from the Bahá'í standpoint they are divorced and may then proceed to seek to obtain a civil divorce. Apart from irretrievable marital breakdown, there are no necessary preconditions for divorce.

As to the procreation of children, this is regarded as the primary purpose of marriage. For this reason, the use of contraception is permitted only in order to limit the total number of children, and not in order to prevent the conception of any children whatsoever, unless this be for medical reasons. Sterilization is also forbidden except where the mother's life may be endangered by pregnancy. Artificial insemination is permitted only when the husband is the father of the child. As to abortion, this is only permitted if there are strong medical reasons for it, and abortion purely for the purpose of getting rid of an unwanted child is prohibited. In practice, however, abortion is regarded as a matter of personal decision, albeit that Bahá'ís believe that the human soul comes into being at the moment of conception. Any consideration of abortion is regarded as a major matter of conscience and not a decision to be taken lightly.

The Bahá'í ideal of family life is that it should be unified and harmonious. Based on the stable marriage of the parents, it should be an integral social unit in which the rights and obligations of each member are respected. Thus, parents are under a spiritual obligation to educate their children and to promote their moral and spiritual training and welfare. They must also ensure that their children learn to read and write. Failure to educate and train one's children is regarded as a sin. For their part, children should respect their parents, obey them and care for them. As between the parents, whilst both are equal and neither should dominate, the father has the primary obligation to support his family and the mother has the primary obligation to raise the children. Neither of these obligations are exclusive. Mutual respect also requires that family differences should be settled by consultation. When the family is united, it will prosper.

Death and Burial

Bahá'ís are advised to prepare for the inevitability of death, both spiritually, by calling themselves to moral account, and materially, by preparing a will.

Bahá'ís believe that as the former resting-place of the soul, the dead body should be treated with respect. Respect entails that the corpse be carefully washed and shrouded before being placed in a fine coffin and buried. Middle Eastern Bahá'ís also place a Bahá'í ring on the hand of the deceased. In marked distinction to the nineteenth-century Iranian Shi'i practice of transporting corpses to far-distant shrines, Bahá'u'lláh stipulated that Bahá'ís should bury their dead at a site no more than an hour's journey from the place of death. There are a number of specific prayers for the dead which may be said at the funeral, and Bahá'ís commonly place over the grave a stone inscribed with some Bahá'í symbol or scriptural verse.

Life-style

The Bahá'í leaders urged their followers to distinguish themselves by their good deeds, their spirituality and their moral rectitude, but otherwise generally discouraged the adoption of any practices which would serve to separate Bahá'ís from other people. Bahá'ís are encouraged to be universalistic in their attitudes and not divisive.

At the same time, however, Bahá'ís are severely critical of what might be termed secular hedonism, and certain Bahá'í injunctions and prohibitions are distinctive in terms of the prevailing mores of modern Western culture. Prominent here are the Bahá'í insistence on the absolute avoidance of pre-marital and extra-marital sex, the prohibitions on gambling and on the use of alcohol and habit-forming drugs, and the condemnation of homosexuality. All of these are emphasized in the Bahá'í writings, and in extreme cases failure to comply with the appropriate Bahá'í standard can lead to administrative sanctions. But beyond these basic principles, Bahá'ís are not strongly puritanical. Individuals are advised to be moderate in their behaviour and to develop their own sense of moral responsibility and judgement.

As regards other aspects of life-style, there are few distinctively Bahá'í practices, and there are no specific Bahá'í food prohibitions, forms of dress or names. Again, whilst 'Abdu'l-Bahá spoke favourably of vegetarianism, and Bahá'ís are advised to be moderate in their dress and (for men) the cut of their hair, these are matters of individual choice, and no pattern of Bahá'í behaviour in these areas has emerged. Tobacco smoking is also discouraged, but it is not forbidden.

The only areas of common Bahá'í practice which are distinctive are the use of Bahá'í symbols and the greeting, *Alláh-u-Abhá* (God is Most Glorious). The Bahá'í symbols are linked to the Islamic tradition that God has a 'greatest name'. Bahá'ís believe that this name is *'Bahá'* (glory, splendour) and use variants of it as a greeting, as a symbol on a Bahá'í ring, and as a distinctive wall-hanging: a calligraphic representation of the Arabic phrase, *Yá-Bahá'u'l-Abhá* (O Thou the Glory of the All-Glorious). The ring symbol (a) and the *Yá Bahá'u'l-Abhá* (b) are shown below.

The number nine (the Arabic numerical equivalent of *Bahá*) has symbolic value and is sometimes used as a decorative motif. Bahá'ís consider it disrespectful to possess pictures of Bahá'u'lláh and normally see these only on the occasion of pilgrimage to

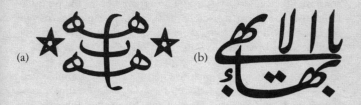

(a)   (b)

Haifa, but many Bahá'ís display photographs of 'Abdu'l-Bahá in their homes.

In terms of artistic products, there are no distinctively Bahá'í forms, but individual Bahá'ís have produced a wide range of music, poetry and painting which have been influenced by Bahá'í themes. Again, Bahá'í architects have sought to represent Bahá'í concepts in their designs for Bahá'í Houses of Worship and other buildings.

Membership of Non-Bahá'í Organizations

When the Bahá'í religion first developed, both in Iran and in the West, membership often tended to be inclusive in nature. Many Bahá'ís retained strong links with their religion of origin and continued to attend their mosque, synagogue or church. This situation only changed at the direction of Shoghi Effendi, and a far more exclusive concept of membership emerged. Accordingly, Bahá'ís are now forbidden to retain dual religious membership. If they are Bahá'ís they should have great respect for other religions, but they are not Buddhists, Hindus, Muslims, Jews or Christians and should not behave as if they were.

Shoghi Effendi also insisted that Bahá'ís should not be accredited members of any secular organization whose goals or methods were incompatible with those of the Bahá'í Faith. He included all political parties within this prohibition, arguing that whilst some political groups might support some Bahá'í principles, none supported them all, and that in any case all parties were by their very nature divisive and hence contrary to the spirit of the Bahá'í teachings. Bahá'ís are also forbidden to be members of secret organizations such as Freemasonry. By contrast, Bahá'ís are welcome to support the work of inter-religious, social or charitable organizations whose goals are compatible with their own, as for example, the Esperantists, the United Nations Association, or the World Congress of Faiths.

Bahá'í Gatherings

Bahá'ís meet for a variety of formal and informal gatherings. The main formal meetings are the Nineteen Day Feasts and the commemoration of Bahá'í Holy Days.

The Nineteen Day Feast may be regarded as the focus of local Bahá'í community life. It is held once in every nineteen days, ideally on the first day of each Bahá'í month (see below). It comprises three sections: a devotional period in which Bahá'í prayers and extracts from the Bahá'í writings are read or chanted; a consultative session in which the community is able to discuss its objectives and plans, and to make recommendations to the local Bahá'í Assembly; and a social section in which refreshments are shared. In larger Bahá'í communities several Feasts may be held for Bahá'ís in different neighbourhoods, but in most local Bahá'í communities only one Feast is held.

The Bahá'í calendar, which regulates the holding of the Nineteen Day Feasts, consists of a year of nineteen months each of nineteen days (= 361 days). There are also four or five intercalary days to bring the Bahá'í year into alignment with the solar year. The months are named after various spiritual qualities or divine names and attributes. They are as follows:

Month		First Day
1	Bahá (Splendour)	21 March
2	Jalál (Glory)	9 April
3	Jamál (Beauty)	28 April
4	'Aẓamat (Grandeur)	17 May
5	Núr (Light)	5 June
6	Raḥmat (Mercy)	24 June
7	Kalimát (Words)	13 July
8	Kamál (Perfection)	1 August

9	Asmá (Names)	20 August
10	'Izzat (Might)	8 September
11	Mashíyyat (Will)	27 September
12	'Ilm (Knowledge)	16 October
13	Qudrat (Power)	4 November
14	Qawl (Speech)	23 November
15	Masá'il (Questions)	12 December
16	Sharaf (Honour)	31 December
17	Sultán (Sovereignty)	19 January
18	Mulk (Dominion)	7 February
19	'Alá' (Loftiness)	2 March

The intercalary days are placed just prior to the month of fasting ('Alá). The Bahá'í New Year coincides with the traditional Persian New Year (*Naw-Rúz*) and is held on the spring equinox (normally 21 March).

The Bahá'í Holy Days commemorate the births, declarations of mission, and deaths of the Báb and Bahá'u'lláh. Naw-Rúz is also celebrated as a Holy Day. These days are all treated as religious holidays and, where possible, Bahá'ís do not work on these days. In addition, Bahá'ís commemorate the death of 'Abdu'l-Bahá and (symbolically) the creation of the Bahá'í Covenant. Commemoratory meetings are held on each of these days, but there is no set form. Generally selections of Bahá'í writings are read and refreshments are served. There may also be music. Celebratory parties are often organized for the New Year and the intercalary days.

The dates of the Holy Days are as follows (those on which Bahá'ís should not work are marked with an asterisk):

*	21 March	Naw-Rúz (New Year)	
*	21 April	1st day of Riḍván	⎫
*	29 April	9th day of Riḍván	⎬ Bahá'u'lláh's declaration of his mission (1863)
*	2 May	12th day of Riḍván	⎭

* 23 May	The Báb's declaration of his mission (1844)
* 29 May	Passing of Bahá'u'lláh (1892)
* 9 July	Martyrdom of the Báb (1850)
* 20 October	Birth of the Báb (1819)
* 12 November	Birth of Bahá'u'lláh (1817)
26 November	Day of the Covenant
28 November	Passing of 'Abdu'l-Bahá (1921)

In addition to these regular formal meetings, individual Bahá'ís and local Bahá'í groups and Assemblies often organize meetings for the study of the Bahá'í writings and teachings, prayer meetings and informal discussion meetings ('firesides') to which they invite those who wish to investigate the Bahá'í Faith. Bahá'í Assemblies and committees also organize regional, national and international conferences to discuss and promote the aims of the Bahá'í Faith. Again, many Bahá'í communities organize residential conferences for the more detailed study of the Bahá'í teachings (summer schools or their equivalent). Many communities also sponsor an annual 'World Religion Day' dedicated to the theme of harmony and understanding between the world's religions. Public meetings and meetings to mark events such as Human Rights Day may also be organized.

Bahá'í Pilgrimage

All Bahá'ís are encouraged to visit the Bahá'í holy places in Haifa and 'Akká. These pilgrimages, and the reports of returning pilgrims, provide an important focus for Bahá'í identity. Most pilgrimages last for nine days and include visits to the shrines of Bahá'u'lláh, the Báb and 'Abdu'l-Bahá; to Bahá'u'lláh's prison cell in 'Akká; to various houses in which Bahá'u'lláh and 'Abdu'l-Bahá lived; and to the Bahá'í Archives Building in which many of the original writings, clothes and personal effects of the Bahá'í leaders are stored. The pilgrims also meet with the members of the Universal House of Justice and of the International Teaching

Centre, and attend lectures, discussions and prayer meetings. As the pilgrim groups are invariably multinational, they provide a basis for a sense of the global solidarity of the Bahá'í community. Many pilgrims also visit the Jewish, Christian and Islamic sites in the Holy Land.

Apart from the pilgrimage to Haifa and 'Akká, many Bahá'ís visit the grave of Shoghi Effendi in London. This is not regarded as a formal pilgrimage but as an act of great devotion. Before the Islamic Revolution in Iran, Bahá'ís also used to visit the various Bahá'í holy places in that country. Many of these have now been expropriated, however, and several have been deliberately destroyed by the authorities.

Bahá'í Buildings

Bahá'ís do not need special churches or temples in order to worship. Their gatherings are often in rented halls or in their own homes. Larger Bahá'í communities often do have their own meeting places, however, and each national community has its own administrative headquarters. There are also the various shrines and holy places, the recently completed (1983) building used by the Universal House of Justice and a number of Bahá'í Houses of Worship.

The House of Worship, or *Mashriqu'l-Adhkár* (dawning-place of the mention of God), is intended to become the spiritual fulcrum of each Bahá'í community, and it is ultimately intended that there should be one in each local Bahá'í community of any size. It is also intended that each House of Worship should be surrounded by a series of educational, medical and humanitarian service buildings. Due to the cost of such constructions, only eight central Houses of Worship have so far been built, essentially on a continental basis. The first of these, in Asiatic Russia, was later expropriated during the Stalinist era and, following earthquake damage, was destroyed by the government authorities. The other seven are in the USA, Panama, West Germany, Uganda, India, Australia and Western Samoa. Two service buildings (homes for the aged) have also been constructed.

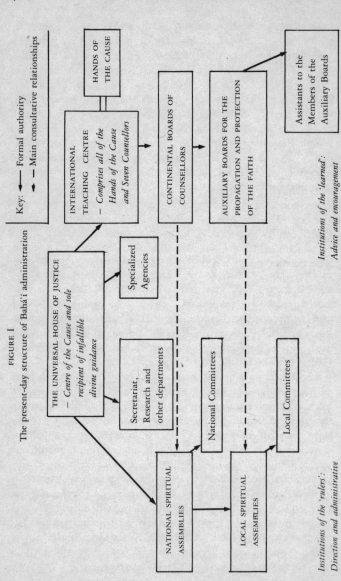

FIGURE I
The present-day structure of Bahá'í administration

Key: —— Formal authority
     – – – Main consultative relationships

HANDS OF
THE CAUSE

INTERNATIONAL
TEACHING CENTRE
– Comprises all of the
Hands of the Cause
and Seven Counsellors

THE UNIVERSAL HOUSE OF JUSTICE
– Centre of the Cause and sole
recipient of infallible
divine guidance

Specialized
Agencies

CONTINENTAL BOARDS OF
COUNSELLORS

AUXILIARY BOARDS FOR THE
PROPAGATION AND PROTECTION
OF THE FAITH

Assistants to the
Members of the
Auxiliary Boards

Secretariat,
Research and
other departments

National Committees

Local Committees

NATIONAL SPIRITUAL
ASSEMBLIES

LOCAL SPIRITUAL
ASSEMBLIES

Institutions of the 'learned':
Advice and encouragement

Institutions of the 'rulers':
Direction and administrative
authority

6

Bahá'í Administration

FOR Bahá'ís, their vision of a new world order receives practical expression in their system of organization. The Bahá'í 'Administrative Order' is seen as a precursor of the world order of the future, and as such its development provides an important means by which the future divine kingdom may be established on earth. The Bahá'í administration is not just a necessary vehicle for the organization of the Bahá'í community. It is regarded as a divinely-ordained system which has been created to channel dynamic spiritual energies towards the re-creation of individuals and, ultimately, of society itself.

The Structure of Bahá'í Administration

The structure of Bahá'í administration, based upon the writings of Bahá'u'lláh, has been considerably developed by the successive leaders of the Bahá'í Faith. Its present-day form is shown in Figure I. The supreme ruling body is now the Universal House of Justice. First established in 1963, the House of Justice is regarded as being the divinely-guided centre of the Bahá'í covenant. At present it consists of a nine-man council directly elected every five years by the members of all Bahá'í National Spiritual Assemblies. It has appointed several committees and departments to assist it in various aspects of its work. Besides providing overall guidance and leadership to the Bahá'í community, the House of Justice is empowered to extend the corpus of Bahá'í law in response to the changing circumstances of human society. The seat of the Universal House of Justice is at the Bahá'í World Centre in Haifa.

Subordinate to the Universal House of Justice are two separate branches of the Bahá'í administration: the 'rulers' and the 'learned'. The 'rulers' are those Bahá'í institutions with executive authority over the direction of the Bahá'í community. These are the Local and National Spiritual Assemblies. These bodies are elected annually and consist of nine-member councils. All adult Bahá'ís of good standing of either sex are eligible for membership. The Local Spiritual Assemblies are elected directly by the adult Bahá'ís of a particular locality. The National Assemblies are elected by a convention of delegates, themselves elected by the mass of the Bahá'ís. These elections are conducted by secret ballot and all electioneering is forbidden. The Assemblies appoint various committees to help them in their work. With the increasing size of the Bahá'í community, additional institutions may well be introduced, as in India, where elected 'State Councils' now form an intermediate administrative tier between the Local and National Assemblies. At present (March 1988) there are a total of 148 National Assemblies and 19,592 Local Assemblies.

The responsibilities of the Spiritual Assemblies include the propagation and protection of the Faith, organization of educational and social development programmes, promotion of Bahá'í literature, collection and disbursement of the Bahá'í Funds, holding Bahá'í meetings, institutes and summer schools, and providing counsel to those in trouble or distress.

The Bahá'í institutions of the 'learned' are primarily charged with the tasks of encouraging and promoting the expansion of the Bahá'í Faith and of defending it against attack. In relationship with the Spiritual Assemblies, however, the 'learned' have only an advisory function, and are now explicitly denied general executive authority. The period of leadership by the Hands of the Cause (1957–63) is regarded as an 'interregnum' between two periods of divinely guided leadership.

Of these various institutions of the learned, the first to be established was the 'Hands of the Cause of God', various prominent individuals being appointed to this rank from the time of Bahá'u'lláh. As the Universal House of Justice has ruled that it lacks the authority to appoint further Hands of the Cause, this institution will in due course cease to exist, many of its functions being taken over by the Continental Boards of Counsellors, first established in 1968. These Boards – now five in number with a total membership of 72 – are responsible for consulting with the various National Assemblies of their area, for gathering information about the 'condition of the Cause', and for financing activities at a continental level. The Continental Boards also appoint and direct 'Auxiliary Boards' (first established in 1954) responsible for liaison with Local Assemblies. The Auxiliary Board Members (622 in 1985) are able to appoint assistants to help them in their work. All these institutions are collectively superintended by the 'International Teaching Centre', established in Haifa in 1973 and directly responsible to the Universal House of Justice.

In addition to this main structure of Bahá'í administration there exist a number of specialist agencies concerned with such matters as contact with the United Nations, the coordination of Bahá'í social and economic development programmes, and the promotion of Bahá'í studies.

In practice, Bahá'ís are advised that the structure of their administration should be transcended by its spirit. Spiritual rather than organizational imperatives should be paramount. Spiritual principles, such as consultation and the right to individual self-expression, should be the central concern of Bahá'í administrators and not the minutiae of administrative practice. More specifically, administrative bodies should resist the temptation to over-administer or over-centralize. Individual initiative and enthusiasm are precious resources and must not be stifled.

The principle of consultation is regarded as crucial both within the various Bahá'í institutions and between the institutions and the generality of the Bahá'ís. Problems should be resolved through consultation. True consultation consists of an open yet disinterested expression of views. Each participant should seek to discover the truth of a matter, avoid preconceived judgements, and speak with courtesy and moderation. The group as a whole should seek to come to a harmonious conclusion. More formally, with reference to the relationship between the institutions and the Bahá'ís as a whole, whilst Shoghi Effendi stressed the authority of the institutions, he also emphasized that the key element was frank and loving consultation and not the exercise of dictatorial control. Institutions should take the Bahá'ís into their confidence, and take every opportunity to solicit their opinions and share with them their hopes and plans as in the regular Nineteen Day Feasts. Again, whilst individual Bahá'ís are encouraged to show due respect for the institutions, they have the right to consult with them, and if needs be to appeal against their decisions, either directly or to a higher level of the administration.

It will be noted that the Bahá'í Faith does not have a priesthood. This is true not only in the sense of there not being anyone to perform special ritual or sacerdotal functions, but also because the prestige of individuals within the Bahá'í administration is consciously de-emphasized. Thus, there is no security of tenure in the various administrative offices. All Local and National Assembly members are subject to yearly election, and even the members of the Universal House of Justice are elected every five years. Similarly, the Counsellors, the Board Members and their assistants, and the members of various Bahá'í committees are only appointed for set periods of office. Again, individual Bahá'í administrators are almost entirely members of corporate groups (Assemblies or Boards) and thus subject to the constraints of their fellows or, in the case of the Assemblies, to the need to make collective decisions. The institutions of the learned, with their greater emphasis on the role of the individual members, are emphatically denied any executive authority.

Bahá'í Activities

At present, the majority of formally-organized Bahá'í activities are concerned with the expansion and consolidation of the Bahá'í community. Expansion centres on the public announcement of the Bahá'í teachings ('proclamation'), the endeavour to attract individuals to become Bahá'ís ('teaching'), and the establishment of new Bahá'í Assemblies and groups. Consolidation centres on the endeavours to increase the level of commitment and knowledge within the Bahá'í community ('deepening') and to ensure that the Bahá'í Assemblies function efficiently and harmoniously. To these various ends, Bahá'ís organize teaching and advertising campaigns, lectures, informal 'fireside' gatherings, prayer and deepening meetings, conferences, summer schools, teaching institutes, children's classes and women's meetings. They also publish an extensive range of literature, secure translations in an increasingly large number of languages (by 1987 Bahá'í literature had been published in 520 languages), and have recently begun to establish a series of Bahá'í radio stations in several parts of the world. It should be noted that, as conversion is regarded as a matter of individual conscience, Bahá'ís are encouraged to be moderate in their 'teaching' activities and not to force their message on unwilling hearers.

Besides these 'primary' activities, Bahá'ís are increasingly involved in promoting the more general aims of their religion, notably their social principles. Prominent here is their support for education, and there were in 1987 a total of 84 Bahá'í schools worldwide. These schools are strictly non-sectarian and are open to individuals of any religious or racial background. In addition, there are various other educational projects, including over five hundred rural 'tutorial schools' providing basic training in literacy, public health and agricultural techniques. Involvement in other aspects of socio-economic development includes work in community development, agriculture and forestry, and health and social services. Bahá'ís in several parts of the world have also been involved in the promotion of the cultural activities of minority groups, such as those of the Amerindians in both North and South America.

Another more general area of activity involves support for the United Nations and its specialized agencies. Beginning in the 1940s, contacts between the Bahá'ís and the United Nations have greatly increased. The 'Bahá'í International Community' now enjoys consultative status as a non-governmental organization with the United Nations Economic and Social Council (ECOSOC) and Children's Fund (UNICEF), as well as association with its Environment Programme (UNEP). Many Bahá'í communities also support the activities of their local United Nations Associations. Through these contacts Bahá'ís are able to promote their social ideals, as well as seeking international sympathy and support for those Bahá'ís suffering persecution.

As emphasis on Bahá'í social principles increases – as evidenced by the recent establishment of the Bahá'í Office for Social and Economic Development (1983) and the promulgation of the Universal House of Justice's *The Promise of World Peace* (1985) – this wider range of activities will undoubtedly multiply.

Appendix

Extracts from the Bahá'í Writings

I Bahá'u'lláh

From The Hidden Words

FROM THE ARABIC

This is that which hath descended from the realm of glory, uttered by the tongue of power and might, and revealed unto the Prophets of old. We have taken the inner essence thereof and clothed it in the garment of brevity, as a token of grace unto the righteous, that they may stand faithful unto the covenant of God, may fulfil in their lives His trust, and in the realm of spirit obtain the gem of Divine virtue.

O Son of Spirit! My first counsel is this: Possess a pure, kindly and radiant heart, that thine may be a sovereignty ancient, imperishable and everlasting.

O Son of Spirit! The best beloved of all things in My sight is Justice; turn not away therefrom if thou desirest Me, and neglect it not that I may confide in thee. By its aid thou shalt see with thine own eyes and not through the eyes of others, and shalt know of thine own knowledge and not through the knowledge of thy neighbour. Ponder this in thy heart; how it behoveth thee to be. Verily justice is My gift to thee and the sign of My loving-kindness. Set it then before thine eyes.

O Son of Man! I loved thy creation, hence I created thee. Wherefore, do thou love Me, that I may name thy name and fill thy soul with the spirit of life.

O Son of Being! Love Me, that I may love thee. If thou lovest Me not, My love can in no wise reach thee. Know this, O servant.

O Son of Man! If thou lovest Me, turn away from thyself; and if thou seekest My pleasure, regard not thine own; that thou mayest die in Me and I may eternally live in thee.

O Son of Man! Breathe not the sins of others so long as thou art thyself a sinner. Shouldst thou transgress this command, accursed wouldst thou be, and to this I bear witness.

O Son of Being! Bring thyself to account each day ere thou art summoned to a reckoning; for death, unheralded, shall come upon thee and thou shalt be called to give account for thy deeds.

O Son of the Supreme! I have made death a messenger of joy to thee. Wherefore dost thou grieve? I made the light to shed on thee its splendour. Why dost thou veil thyself therefrom?

O Son of Man! Wert thou to speed through the immensity of space and traverse the expanse of heaven, yet thou shouldst find no rest save in submission to Our Command and humbleness before Our Face.

O Son of Man! Humble thyself before Me, that I may graciously visit thee. Arise for the triumph of My cause, that while yet on earth thou mayest obtain the victory.

O Son of Man! For everything there is a sign. The sign of love is fortitude under My decree and patience under My trials.

O Son of Man! If adversity befall thee not in My path, how canst thou walk in the ways of them that are content with My pleasure? If trials afflict thee not in thy longing to meet Me, how wilt thou attain the light in thy love for My beauty?

O Son of Being! Busy not thyself with this world, for with fire We test the gold, and with gold We test Our servants.

O Son of Beauty! By My spirit and by My favour! By My mercy and by My beauty! All that I have revealed unto thee, with the tongue of power, and have written for thee with the pen of might, hath been in accordance with thy capacity and understanding, not with My state and the melody of My voice.

O Children of Men! Know ye not why We created you all from the same dust? That no one should exalt himself over the other. Ponder at all times in your hearts how ye were created. Since We have created you all from one same substance it is incumbent on you to be even as one soul, to walk with the same feet, eat with the same mouth and dwell in the same land, that from your inmost being, by your deeds and actions, the signs of oneness and the essence of detachment may be made manifest. Such is My counsel to you, O concourse of light! Heed ye this counsel that ye may obtain the fruit of holiness from the tree of wondrous glory.

FROM THE PERSIAN

O Ye People that have Minds to Know and Ears to Hear! The first call of the Beloved is this: O mystic nightingale! Abide not but in the rose-garden of the spirit. O messenger of the Solomon of love! Seek thou no shelter except in the Sheba of the well-beloved, and O immortal phoenix! dwell not save on the mount of faithfulness. Therein is thy habitation, if on the wings of thy soul thou soarest to the realm of the infinite and seekest to attain thy goal.

O Friend! In the garden of thy heart plant naught but the rose of love, and from the nightingale of affection and desire loosen not thy hold. Treasure the companionship of the righteous and eschew all fellowship with the ungodly.

O Son of Justice! Whither can a lover go but to the land of his beloved? and what seeker findeth rest away from his heart's desire? To the true lover reunion is life, and separation is death. His breast is void of patience and his heart hath no peace. A myriad lives he would forsake to hasten to the abode of his beloved.

O Son of Dust! Verily I say unto thee of all men the most negligent is he that disputeth idly and seeketh to advance himself over his brother. Say, O brethren! Let deeds, not words, be your adorning.

O Son of Earth! Know, verily, the heart wherein the least remnant of envy yet lingers, shall never attain My everlasting dominion, nor inhale the sweet savours of holiness breathing from My kingdom of sanctity.

O Friends! Abandon not the everlasting beauty for a beauty that must die, and set not your affections on this mortal world of dust.

O Ye Dwellers in the Highest Paradise! Proclaim unto the children of assurance that within the realms of holiness, nigh unto the celestial paradise, a new garden hath appeared, round which circle the denizens of the realm on high and the immortal dwellers of the exalted paradise. Strive, then, that ye may attain that station, that ye may unravel the mysteries of love from its wind-flowers and learn the secret of divine and consummate wisdom from its eternal fruits. Solaced are the eyes of them that enter and abide therein!

O My Servant! Free thyself from the fetters of this world, and loose thy Soul from the prison of self. Seize thy chance, for it will come to thee no more.

O Companion of My Throne! Hear no evil, and see no evil, abase not thyself, neither sigh and weep. Speak no evil, that thou mayest not hear it spoken unto thee, and magnify not the faults of others that thine own faults may not appear great; and wish not the abasement of anyone, that thine own abasement be not exposed. Live then the days of thy life, that are less than a fleeting moment, with thy mind stainless, thy heart unsullied, thy thoughts pure, and thy nature sanctified, so that, free and content, thou mayest put away this mortal frame and repair unto the mystic paradise, and abide in the eternal kingdom for evermore.

O Quintessence of Passion! Put away all covetousness and seek contentment; for the covetous hath ever been deprived, and the contented hath ever been loved and praised.

O Ye that Pride Yourselves on Mortal Riches! Know ye in truth that wealth is a mighty barrier between the seeker and his desire, the lover and his beloved. The rich, but for a few, shall in no wise attain the court of His presence nor enter the city of content and resignation. Well is it then with him, who being rich, is not hindered by his riches from the eternal kingdom, nor deprived by them of imperishable dominion. By the most great name! The splendour of such a wealthy man shall illuminate the dwellers of heaven, even as the sun enlightens the people of the earth!

O Son of My Handmaid! Guidance hath ever been given by words, and now it is given by deeds. Everyone must show forth deeds that are pure and holy, for words are the property of all alike, whereas such deeds as these belong only to Our loved ones. Strive then with heart and soul to distinguish yourselves by your deeds. In this wise We counsel you in this holy and resplendent tablet.[27]

From The Book of Certitude

O My brother! When a true seeker determineth to take the step of search in the path leading unto the knowledge of the Ancient of Days, he must, before all else, cleanse his heart, which is the seat of the revelation of the inner mysteries of God, from the obscuring dust of all acquired knowledge, and the allusions of the embodiments of satanic fancy. He must purge his breast, which is the sanctuary of the abiding love of the Beloved, of every defilement, and sanctify his soul from all that pertaineth to water and clay, from all shadowy and ephemeral attachments. He must so cleanse his heart that no remnant of either love or hate may linger therein, lest that love blindly incline him to error, or that hate repel him away from the truth. Even as thou dost witness in this Day how most of the people, because of such love and hate, are bereft of the immortal Face, have strayed far from the Embodiments of the Divine mysteries, and, shepherdless, are roaming through the wilderness of oblivion and error.

That seeker must, at all times, put his trust in God, must renounce the peoples of the earth, must detach himself from the world of dust, and cleave unto Him Who is the Lord of Lords. He must never seek to exalt himself above any one, must wash away from the tablet of his heart every trace of pride and vain-glory, must cling unto patience and resignation, observe silence and refrain from idle talk. For the tongue is a smouldering fire, and excess of speech a deadly poison. Material fire consumeth the body, whereas the fire of the tongue devoureth both heart and soul. The force of the former lasteth but for a time, whilst the effects of the latter endureth a century.

That seeker should, also, regard backbiting as grievous error, and keep himself aloof from its dominion, inasmuch as backbiting quencheth the light of the heart, and extinguisheth the life of the soul. He should be content with little, and be freed from all inordinate desire. He should treasure the companionship of them that have renounced the world, and regard avoidance of boastful and worldly people a precious benefit. At the dawn of every day he should commune with God, and, with all his soul, persevere in the quest of his Beloved. He should consume every wayward thought with the flame of His loving mention, and, with the swiftness of lightning, pass by all else save Him. He should succour the dispossessed, and never withhold his favour from the destitute. He should show kindness to animals, how much more unto his fellow-man, to him who is endowed with the power of utterance. He should not hesitate to offer up his life for his Beloved, nor allow the censure of the people to turn him away from the Truth. He should not wish for others that which he doth not wish for himself, nor promise that which he doth not fulfil. With all his heart he should avoid fellowship with evil-doers, and pray for the remission of their sins. He should forgive the sinful, and never despise his low estate, for none knoweth what his own end shall be. How often hath a sinner attained, at the hour of death, to the essence of faith, and, quaffing the immortal draught, hath taken his flight unto the Concourse on high! And how often hath a devout believer, at the hour of his soul's ascension, been so changed as to fall into the nethermost fire!

Our purpose in revealing these convincing and weighty utterances is to impress upon the seeker that he should regard all else beside God as transient, and count all things save Him, Who is the Object of all adoration, as utter nothingness.

These are among the attributes of the exalted, and constitute the hallmark of the spiritually-minded. They have already been mentioned in connection with the requirements of the wayfarers that tread the path of Positive Knowledge. When the detached wayfarer and sincere seeker hath fulfilled these essential conditions, then and only then can he be called a true seeker. Whensoever he hath fulfilled the conditions implied in the verse: 'Whoso maketh efforts for Us,' he shall enjoy the blessings conferred by the words: 'In Our Ways shall We assuredly guide him.' (Qur'án 29:69)

Only when the lamp of search, of earnest striving, of longing desire, of passionate devotion, of fervid love, of rapture, and ecstasy, is kindled within the seeker's heart, and the breeze of His loving-kindness is wafted upon his soul, will the darkness of error be dispelled, the mists of doubts and misgivings be dissipated, and the lights of knowledge and certitude envelop his being. At that hour will the Mystic Herald, bearing the joyful tidings of the Spirit, shine forth from the City of God resplendent as the morn, and through the trumpet-blast of knowledge, will awaken the heart, the soul, and the spirit from the slumber of heedlessness. Then will the manifold favours and outpouring grace of the holy and everlasting Spirit confer such new life upon the seeker that he will find himself endowed with a new eye, a new ear, a new heart, and a new mind. He will contemplate the manifest signs of the universe, and will penetrate the hidden mysteries of the soul. Gazing with the eye of God, he will perceive within every atom a door that leadeth him to the stations of absolute certitude. He will discover in all things the mysteries of Divine Revelation, and the evidences of an everlasting Manifestation.

I swear by God! Were he that treadeth the path of guidance and seeketh to scale the heights of righteousness to attain unto this glorious and exalted station, he would inhale, at a distance of a thousand leagues, the fragrance of God, and would perceive the resplendent morn of a

Divine guidance rising above the Day Spring of all things. Each and every thing, however small, would be to him a revelation, leading him to his Beloved, the Object of his quest. So great shall be the discernment of this seeker that he will discriminate between truth and falsehood, even as he doth distinguish the sun from shadow. If in the uttermost corners of the East the sweet savours of God be wafted, he will assuredly recognize and inhale their fragrance, even though he be dwelling in the uttermost ends of the West. He will, likewise, clearly distinguish all the signs of God — His wondrous utterances, His great works, and mighty deeds — from the doings, the words and ways of men, even as the jeweller who knoweth the gem from the stone, or the man who distinguisheth the spring from autumn, and heat from cold. When the channel of the human soul is cleansed of all worldly and impeding attachments, it will unfailingly perceive the breath of the Beloved across immeasurable distances, and will, led by its perfume, attain and enter the City of Certitude.

Therein he will discern the wonders of His ancient Wisdom, and will perceive all the hidden teachings from the rustling leaves of the Tree that flourisheth in that City. With both his inner and outer ear, he will hear from its dust the hymns of glory and praise ascending unto the Lord of Lords, and with his inner eye will he discover the mysteries of 'return' and 'revival'.

How unspeakably glorious are the signs, the tokens, the revelations, and splendours which He, Who is the King of Names and Attributes, hath destined for that City! The attainment unto this City quencheth thirst without water, and kindleth the love of God without fire. Within every blade of grass are enshrined the mysteries of an inscrutable Wisdom, and upon every rose-bush a myriad nightingales pour out, in blissful rapture, their melody. Its wondrous tulips unfold the mystery of the undying Fire in the Burning Bush, and its sweet savours of holiness breathe the perfume of the Messianic Spirit. It bestoweth wealth without gold, and conferreth immortality without death. In each one of its leaves ineffable delights are treasured, and within every chamber unnumbered mysteries lie hidden.

They that valiantly labour in quest of God, will, when once they have renounced all else but Him, be so attached and wedded unto that City, that a moment's separation from it would to them be unthinkable. They will hearken unto infallible proofs from the Hyacinth of that assembly, and will receive the surest testimonies from the beauty of its Rose, and the melody of its Nightingale. Once in about a thousand years shall this City be renewed and readorned . . .

That City is none other than the Word of God revealed in every age and dispensation. In the days of Moses it was the Pentateuch; in the days of Jesus, the Gospel; in the days of Muḥammad, the Messenger of God, the Qur'án; in this day, the Bayán; and in the Dispensation of Him Whom God will make manifest, His own Book – the Book unto which all the Books of former Dispensations must needs be referred, the Book that standeth amongst them all transcendent and supreme.[28]

From Bahá'u'lláh's Proclamation to the Kings and Leaders of Religion

O Kings of the earth! Give ear unto the Voice of God, calling from this sublime, this fruit-laden Tree, that hath sprung out of the Crimson Hill, upon the holy Plain, intoning the words: 'There is none other God but He, the Mighty, the All-Powerful, the All-Wise.' . . . Fear God, O concourse of kings, and suffer not yourselves to be deprived of this most sublime grace. Fling away, then, the things ye possess, and take fast hold on the Handle of God, the Exalted, the Great. Set your hearts towards the Face of God, and abandon that which your desires have bidden you to follow, and be not of those who perish. Relate unto them, O servant, the story of 'Alí (the Báb), when He came unto them with truth, bearing His glorious and weighty Book, and holding in His hands a testimony and proof from God, and holy and blessed tokens from Him. Ye, however, O kings, have failed to heed the Remembrance of God in His days and to be guided by the lights which arose and shone forth above the horizon of a resplendent Heaven. Ye examined not His Cause when so to do would have been better for you than all that the sun shineth upon, could ye but perceive it. Ye remained careless until the divines of Persia – those cruel ones – pronounced judgement against Him, and unjustly slew Him. His spirit ascended unto God, and the eyes of the inmates of Paradise and the angels that are nigh unto Him wept sore by reason of this cruelty. Beware that ye be not careless henceforth as ye have been careless aforetime. Return, then, unto God, your Maker, and be not of the heedless . . . My face hath come forth from the veils, and shed its radiance upon all that is in heaven and on earth; and yet, ye turned not towards Him, notwithstanding that ye were created for Him, O concourse of kings! Follow, therefore, that which I speak unto you, and hearken unto it with your hearts, and be not of such as have turned aside. For your glory consisteth not in your sovereignty, but rather in your nearness unto God and your observance of His command as sent down in His holy and preserved Tablets. Should any one of you rule over the whole earth, and over all that lieth within it and upon it, its seas, its lands, its mountains, and its plains, and yet be not remembered by God, all these would profit him not, could ye but know it . . . Arise, then, and make steadfast your feet, and make ye amends for that which hath escaped you, and set then yourselves towards His holy Court, on the shore of His mighty Ocean, so that the pearls of knowledge and wisdom, which God hath stored up within the shell of His radiant heart, may be revealed unto you . . . Beware lest ye hinder the breeze of God from blowing over your hearts, the breeze through which the hearts of such as have turned unto Him can be quickened . . .

O kings of Christendom! Heard ye not the saying of Jesus, the Spirit of God, 'I go away, and come again unto you'? Wherefore, then, did ye fail, when He did come again unto you in the clouds of heaven, to draw nigh unto Him, that ye might behold His face, and be of them that attained His Presence? In another passage He saith: 'When He, the Spirit of Truth, is come, He will guide you into all truth.' And yet, behold how, when He did bring the truth, ye refused to turn your faces towards Him, and persisted in disporting yourselves with your pastimes and fancies. Ye welcomed Him not, neither did ye seek His Presence, that ye might hear the verses of God from His own mouth, and partake of the manifold wisdom of the Almighty, the All-Glorious, the All-Wise. Ye have, by reason of your failure, hindered the breath of God from being wafted over you, and have withheld from your souls the sweetness of its fragrance. Ye continue roving with delight in the valley of your corrupt desires. Ye, and all ye possess, shall pass away. Ye shall, most certainly, return to God, and shall be called to account for your doings in the presence of Him Who shall gather together the entire creation . . .

God hath committed into your hands the reins of the government of the people, that ye may rule with justice over them, safeguard the rights of the down-trodden, and punish the wrongdoers. If ye neglect the duty prescribed unto you by God in His Book, your names shall be numbered with those of the unjust in His sight. Grievous, indeed, will be your error. Cleave ye to that which your imaginations have devised, and cast behind your backs the commandments of God, the Most Exalted, the Inaccessible, the All-Compelling, the Almighty? Cast away the things ye possess, and cling to that which God hath bidden you observe. Seek ye His grace, for he that seeketh it treadeth His straight Path . . .

Lay not aside the fear of God, O kings of the earth, and beware that ye transgress not the bounds which the Almighty hath fixed. Observe the injunctions laid upon you in His Book, and take good heed not to overstep their limits. Be vigilant, that ye may not do injustice to anyone, be it to the extent of a grain of mustard seed. Tread ye the path of justice, for this, verily, is the straight path.

Compose your differences, and reduce your armaments, that the burden of your expenditures may be lightened, and that your minds and hearts may be tranquillized. Heal the dissensions that divide you, and ye will no longer be in need of any armaments except what the protection of your cities and territories demandeth. Fear ye God, and take heed not to outstrip the bounds of moderation, and be numbered among the extravagant.

We have learned that you are increasing your outlay every year, and are laying the burden thereof on your subjects. This, verily, is more than they can bear, and is a grievous injustice. Decide justly between men, and be ye the emblems of justice amongst them. This if ye judge fairly, is the thing that behoveth you, and beseemeth your station.

Beware not to deal unjustly with any one that appealeth to you, and entereth beneath your shadow. Walk ye in the fear of God, and be ye of them that lead a godly life. Rest not on your power, your armies and treasures. Put your whole trust and confidence in God, Who hath created you, and seek ye His help in all your affairs. Succour cometh from Him alone. He succoureth whom He will with the hosts of the heavens and of the earth.

Know ye that the poor are the trust of God in your midst. Watch that ye betray not His trust, that ye deal not unjustly with them and that ye walk not in the ways of the treacherous. Ye will most certainly be called upon to answer for His trust on the day when the Balance of Justice shall be set, the day when unto every one shall be rendered his due, when the doings of all men, be they rich or poor, shall be weighed.

If ye pay no heed unto the counsels which, in peerless and unequivocal language, We have revealed in this Tablet, Divine chastisement shall assail you from every direction, and the sentence of His justice shall be pronounced against you. On that day ye shall have no power to resist Him, and shall recognize your own impotence. Have mercy on yourselves and on those beneath you. Judge ye between them according to the precepts prescribed by God in His most holy and exalted Tablet, a Tablet wherein He hath assigned to each and every thing its settled measure, in which He hath given, with distinctness, an explanation of all things, and which is in itself a monition unto them that believe in Him.

Examine Our Cause, inquire into the things that have befallen Us, and decide justly between Us and Our enemies, and be ye of them that act equitably towards their neighbour. If ye stay not the hand of the oppressor, if ye fail to safeguard the rights of the down-trodden, what right have ye then to vaunt yourselves among men? What is it of which ye can rightly boast? Is it on your food and your drink that ye pride yourselves, on the riches ye lay up in your treasuries, on the diversity and the cost of the ornaments with which ye deck yourselves? If true glory were to consist in the possession of such perishable things, then the earth on which ye walk must needs vaunt itself over you, because it supplieth you, and bestoweth upon you, these very things, by the decree of the Almighty. In its bowels are contained, according to what God hath ordained, all that ye possess. From it, as a sign of His mercy, ye derive your riches. Behold then your state, the thing in which ye glory! Would that ye could perceive it!

Nay! By Him Who holdeth in His grasp the kingdom of the entire creation! Nowhere doth your true and abiding glory reside except in your firm adherence unto the precepts of God, your whole-hearted observance of His laws, your resolution to see that they do not remain unenforced, and to pursue steadfastly the right course.[29]

From the letter to Queen Victoria

O Queen in London! Incline thine ear unto the voice of thy Lord, the Lord of all mankind, calling from the Divine Lote-Tree: Verily, no God is there but Me, the Almighty, the All-Wise. Cast away all that is on earth, and attire the head of thy kingdom with the crown of the remembrance of thy Lord, the All-Glorious. He, in truth, hath come unto the world in His most great glory, and all that hath been mentioned in the Gospel hath been fulfilled. The land of Syria hath been honoured by the footsteps of its Lord, the Lord of all men, and North and South are both inebriated with the wine of His presence. Blessed is the man that inhaled the fragrance of the Most Merciful, and turned unto the Dawning-Place of His Beauty, in this resplendent Dawn . . .

Lay aside thy desire, and set then thine heart towards thy Lord, the Ancient of Days. We make mention of thee for the sake of God, and desire that thy name may be exalted through thy remembrance of God, the Creator of earth and heaven. He, verily, is witness unto that which I say. We have been informed that thou hast forbidden the trading in slaves, both men and women. This, verily, is what God hath enjoined in this wondrous Revelation. God hath, truly, destined a reward for thee, because of this. He, verily, will pay the doer of good his due recompense, wert thou to follow what hath been sent unto thee by Him Who is the All-Knowing, the All-Informed. As to him who turneth aside, and swelleth with pride after that the clear tokens have come unto him, from the Revealer of signs, his work shall God bring to naught. He, in truth, hath power over all things. Man's actions are acceptable after his having recognized (the Manifestation). He that turneth aside from the True One is indeed the most veiled amongst His creatures. Thus hath it been decreed by Him Who is the Almighty, the Most Powerful.

We have also heard that thou hast entrusted the reins of counsel into the hands of the representatives of the people. Thou, indeed, hast done well, for thereby the foundations of the edifice of thine affairs will be strengthened, and the hearts of all that are beneath thy shadow, whether high or low, will be tranquillized. It behoveth them, however, to be trustworthy among His servants, and to regard themselves as the representatives of all that dwell on earth. This is what counselleth them, in this Tablet, He Who is the Ruler, the All-Wise . . . Blessed is he that entereth the assembly for the sake of God, and judgeth between men with pure justice. He, indeed, is of the blissful.

O ye the elected representatives of the people in every land! Take ye counsel together, and let your concern be only for that which profiteth mankind, and bettereth the condition thereof, if ye be of them that scan heedfully. Regard the world as the human body which, though at its creation whole and perfect, hath been afflicted, through various causes, with grave disorders and maladies. Not for one day did it gain ease, nay its sickness waxed more severe, as it fell under the treatment of ignorant physicians, who gave full rein to their personal desires, and have erred grievously. And if, at one time, through the care of an able physician, a member of that body was healed, the rest remained afflicted as before. Thus informeth you the All-Knowing, the All-Wise.

We behold it, in this day, at the mercy of rulers so drunk with pride that they cannot discern clearly their own best advantage, much less recognize a Revelation so bewildering and challenging as this. And whenever any one of them hath striven to improve its condition, his motive hath been his own gain, whether confessedly so or not; and the unworthiness of this motive hath limited his power to heal or cure.

That which the Lord hath ordained as the sovereign remedy and mightiest instrument for the healing of all the world is the union of all its peoples in one universal Cause, one common Faith. This can in no wise be achieved except through the power of a skilled, an all-powerful and inspired Physician. This, verily, is the truth, and all else naught but error . . .

O ye rulers of the earth! Wherefore have ye clouded the radiance of the Sun, and caused it to cease from shining? Hearken unto the counsel given you by the Pen of the Most High, that haply both ye and the poor may attain unto tranquillity and peace. We beseech God to assist the kings of the earth to establish peace on earth. He, verily, doth what He willeth.

O kings of the earth! We see you increasing every year your expenditures, and laying the burden thereof on your subjects. This, verily, is wholly and grossly unjust. Fear the sighs and tears of this Wronged One, and lay not excessive burdens on your peoples. Do not rob them to rear palaces for yourselves; nay rather choose for them that which ye choose for yourselves. Thus We unfold to your eyes that which profiteth you, if ye but perceive. Your people are your treasures. Beware lest your rule violate the commandments of God, and ye deliver your wards to the hands of the robber. By them ye rule, by their means ye subsist, by their aid ye conquer. Yet, how disdainfully ye look upon them! How strange, how very strange!

Now that ye have refused the Most Great Peace, hold ye fast unto this, the Lesser Peace, that haply ye may in some degree better your own condition and that of your dependents.

O rulers of the earth! Be reconciled among yourselves, that ye may need no more armaments save in a measure to safeguard your territories and dominions. Beware lest ye disregard the counsel of the All-Knowing, the Faithful.

Be united, O kings of the earth, for thereby will the tempest of discord be stilled amongst you, and your peoples find rest, if ye be of them that comprehend. Should any one among you take up arms against another, rise ye all against him, for this is naught but manifest justice . . .[30]

From The Most Holy Book

The first duty prescribed by God for His servants is the recognition of Him Who is the Day Spring of His Revelation and the Fountain of His laws, Who representeth the Godhead in both the Kingdom of His Cause and the world of creation. Whoso achieveth this duty hath attained unto all good; and whoso is deprived thereof, hath gone astray, though he be the author of every righteous deed. It behoveth every one who reacheth this most sublime station, this summit of transcendent glory, to observe every ordinance of Him Who is the Desire of the world. These twin duties are inseparable. Neither is acceptable without the other. Thus hath it been decreed by Him Who is the Source of Divine inspiration.

They whom God hath endued with insight will readily recognize that the precepts laid down by God constitute the highest means for the maintenance of order in the world and the security of its peoples. He that turneth away from them, is accounted among the abject and foolish. We verily, have commanded you to refuse the dictates of your evil passions and corrupt desires, and not to transgress the bounds which the Pen of the Most High hath fixed, for these are the breath of life unto all created things. The seas of Divine wisdom and divine utterance have risen under the breath of the breeze of the All-Merciful. Hasten to drink your fill, O men of understanding! They that have violated the Covenant of God by breaking His commandments, and have turned back on their heels, these have erred grievously in the sight of God, the All-Possessing, the Most High.

O ye peoples of the world! Know assuredly that My commandments are the lamps of My loving providence among My servants, and the keys of My mercy for My creatures. Thus hath it been sent down from the heaven of the Will of your Lord, the Lord of Revelation. Were any man to taste the sweetness of the words which the lips of the All-Merciful have willed to utter, he would, though the treasures of the earth be in his possession, renounce them one and all, that he might vindicate the truth of even one of His commandments shining above the day spring of His bountiful care and loving-kindness.

Say: From My laws the sweet smelling savour of My garment can be smelled, and by their aid the standards of Victory will be planted upon the highest peaks. The Tongue of My power hath, from the heaven of My omnipotent glory, addressed to My creation these words: 'Observe My commandments, for the love of My beauty.' Happy is the lover that hath inhaled the divine fragrance of his Best-Beloved from these words, laden with the perfume of a grace which no tongue can describe. By My life! He who hath drunk the choice wine of fairness from the hands of My bountiful favour, will circle around My commandments that shine above the Day Spring of My creation.

Think not that We have revealed unto you a mere code of laws. Nay, rather, We have unsealed the choice Wine with the fingers of might and power. To this beareth witness that which the Pen of Revelation hath revealed. Meditate upon this, O men of insight! . . .

Whenever My laws appear like the sun in the heaven of Mine utterance, they must be faithfully obeyed by all, though My decree be such as to cause the heaven of every religion to be cleft asunder. He doth what He pleaseth. He chooseth; and none may question His choice. Whatsoever He, the Well-Beloved, ordaineth, the same is, verily, beloved. To this He Who is the Lord of all creation beareth Me witness. Whoso hath inhaled the sweet fragrance of the All-Merciful, and recognized the Source of this utterance, will welcome with his own eyes the shafts of the enemy, that he may establish the truth of the laws of God amongst men. Well is it with him that hath turned thereunto, and apprehended the meaning of His decisive decree.[31]

Consider the pettiness of men's minds. They ask for that which injureth them, and cast away the thing that profiteth them. They are, indeed, of those that are far astray. We find some men desiring liberty, and priding themselves therein. Such men are in the depths of ignorance.

Liberty must, in the end, lead to sedition, whose flames none can quench. Thus warneth you He Who is the Reckoner, the All-Knowing. Know ye that the embodiment of liberty and its symbol is the animal. That which beseemeth man is submission unto such restraints as will protect him from his own ignorance, and guard him against the harm of the mischief-maker. Liberty causeth man to overstep the bounds of propriety, and to infringe on the dignity of his station. It debaseth him to the level of extreme depravity and wickedness.

Regard men as a flock of sheep that need a shepherd for their protection. This, verily, is the truth, the certain truth. We approve of liberty in certain circumstances, and refuse to sanction it in others. We, verily, are the All-Knowing.

Say: True liberty consisteth in man's submission unto My commandments, little as ye know it. Were men to observe that which We have sent down unto them from the Heaven of Revelation, they would, of a certainty, attain unto perfect liberty. Happy is the man that hath apprehended the Purpose of God in whatever He hath revealed from the Heaven of His Will, that pervadeth all created things. Say: The liberty that profiteth you is to be found nowhere except in complete servitude unto God, the Eternal Truth. Whoso hath tasted of its sweetness will refuse to barter it for all the dominion of earth and heaven.[32]

From Splendours (Ishráqát)

He whom the world hath wronged now proclaimeth: The light of Justice is dimmed, and the sun of Equity veiled from sight. The robber occupieth the seat of the protector and guard, and the position of the faithful is seized by the traitor. A year ago an oppressor ruled over this city, and at every instant caused fresh harm. By the righteousness of the Lord! He wrought that which cast terror into the hearts of men. But to the Pen of Glory the tyranny of the world hath never been nor will it ever be a hindrance. In the abundance of Our grace and loving-kindness We have revealed specially for the rulers and ministers of the world that which is conducive to safety and protection, tranquillity and peace; haply the children of men may rest secure from the evils of oppression. He, verily, is the Protector, the Helper, the Giver of victory. It is incumbent upon the men of God's House of Justice to fix their gaze by day and by night upon that which hath shone forth from the Pen of Glory for the training of peoples, the upbuilding of nations, the protection of man and the safeguarding of his honour.

THE FIRST ISHRÁQ

When the Day-Star of Wisdom rose above the horizon of God's Holy

Dispensation it voiced this all-glorious utterance: They that are possessed of wealth and invested with authority and power must show the profoundest regard for religion. In truth, religion is a radiant light and an impregnable stronghold for the protection and welfare of the peoples of the world, for the fear of God impelleth man to hold fast to that which is good, and shun all evil. Should the lamp of religion be obscured, chaos and confusion will ensue, and the lights of fairness and justice, of tranquillity and peace cease to shine. Unto this will bear witness every man of true understanding.

THE SECOND ISHRÁQ

We have enjoined upon all mankind to establish the Lesser Peace — the surest of all means for the protection of humanity. The sovereigns of the world should, with one accord, hold fast thereunto, for this is the supreme instrument that can ensure the security and welfare of all peoples and nations. They, verily, are the manifestations of the power of God and the dayprings of His authority. We beseech the Almighty that He may graciously assist them in that which is conducive to the well-being of their subjects . . .

THE THIRD ISHRÁQ

It is incumbent upon everyone to observe God's holy commandments, inasmuch as they are the wellspring of life unto the world. The heaven of divine wisdom is illumined with the two luminaries of consultation and compassion and the canopy of world order is upraised upon the two pillars of reward and punishment.

THE FOURTH ISHRÁQ

In this Revelation the hosts that can render it victorious are the hosts of praiseworthy deeds and upright character. The leader and commander of these hosts hath ever been the fear of God, a fear that encompasseth all things and reigneth over all things.

THE FIFTH ISHRÁQ

Governments should fully acquaint themselves with the conditions of those they govern, and confer upon them positions according to desert and merit. It is enjoined upon every ruler and sovereign to consider this matter with the utmost care that the traitor may not usurp the position of the faithful, nor the despoiler rule in the place of the trustworthy . . .

THE SIXTH ISHRÁQ

is union and concord amongst the children of men. From the beginning of time the light of unity hath shed its divine radiance upon the world, and the greatest means for the promotion of that unity is for the peoples of the world to understand one another's writing and speech. In former Epistles We have enjoined upon the Trustees of the House of Justice either to choose one language from among those now existing or to adopt a new one, and in like manner to select a common script, both of which should be taught in all the schools of the world. Thus will the earth be regarded as one country and one home. The most glorious fruit of the tree of knowledge is this exalted word: Of one tree are all ye the fruit, and of one bough the leaves. Let not man glory in this that ye loveth his country, let him rather glory in this that he loveth his kind . . .

THE SEVENTH ISHRÁQ

The Pen of Glory counselleth everyone regarding the instruction and education of children. Behold that which the Will of God hath revealed upon Our arrival in the Prison City and recorded in the Most Holy Book (*Kitáb-i-Aqdas*). Unto every father hath been enjoined the instruction of his son and daughter in the art of reading and writing and in all that hath been laid down in the Holy Tablet. He that putteth away that which is commanded unto him, the Trustees are then to take from him that which is required for their instruction, if he be wealthy, and if not the matter devolveth upon the House of Justice. Verily, have We made it a shelter for the poor and needy. He that bringeth up his son or the son of another, it is as though he hath brought up a son of Mine; upon him rest My Glory, My Loving-Kindness, My Mercy, that have compassed the world.

THE EIGHTH ISHRÁQ

This passage, now written by the Pen of Glory, is accounted as part of the Most Holy Book: The men of God's House of Justice have been charged with the affairs of the people. They, in truth, are the Trustees of God among His servants and the daysprings of authority in His countries.

O people of God! That which traineth the world is Justice, for it is upheld by two pillars, reward and punishment. These two pillars are the sources of life to the world. Inasmuch as for each day there is a new problem and for every problem an expedient solution, such affairs should be referred to the House of Justice that the members thereof may act according to the needs and requirements of the time. They that, for the sake of God, arise to serve His Cause, are the recipients of divine inspiration from the unseen Kingdom. It is incumbent upon all to be obedient unto them. All matters of State should be referred to the House of Justice, but acts of worship must be observed according to that which God hath revealed in His Book.

O people of Bahá! Ye are the dawning-places of the love of God and the daysprings of His loving-kindness. Defile not your tongues with the cursing and reviling of any soul, and guard your eyes against that which is not seemly. Set forth that which ye possess. If it be favourably received, your end is attained; if not, to protest is vain. Leave that soul to himself and turn unto the Lord, the Protector, the Self-Subsisting. Be not the cause of grief, much less of discord and strife. The hope is cherished that ye may obtain true education in the shelter of the tree of His tender mercies and act in accordance with that which God desireth. Ye are all the leaves of one tree and the drops of one ocean.

THE NINTH ISHRÁQ

The purpose of religion as revealed from the heaven of God's holy Will is to establish unity and concord amongst the peoples of the world; make it not the cause of dissension and strife. The religion of God and His divine law are the most potent instruments and the surest of all means for the dawning of the light of unity amongst men. The progress of the world, the development of nations, the tranquillity of peoples, and the peace of all who dwell on earth are among the principles and ordinances of God. Religion bestoweth upon man the most precious of all gifts, offereth the cup of prosperity, imparteth eternal life, and showereth imperishable benefits upon mankind. It behoveth the chiefs and rulers of the world, and in particular the Trustees of God's House of Justice, to endeavour to the utmost of their power to safeguard its position, promote its interests and exalt its station in the eyes of the world. In like manner it is incumbent upon them to enquire into the conditions of their subjects and to acquaint themselves with the affairs and activities of the divers communities in their dominions. We call upon the manifestations of the power of God — the sovereigns and rulers on earth — to bestir themselves and do all in their power that haply they may banish discord from this world and illumine it with the light of concord.

It is incumbent upon everyone to firmly adhere to and observe that which hath streamed forth from Our Most Exalted Pen. God, the True One, beareth Me witness, and every atom in existence is moved to testify that such means as lead to the elevation, the advancement, the education, the protection and the regeneration of the peoples of the earth have been clearly set forth by Us and are revealed in the Holy Books and Tablets by the Pen of Glory.[33]

Some Meditations

Lauded and glorified art Thou, O Lord, my God! How can I make mention of Thee, assured as I am that no tongue, however deep its wisdom, can befittingly magnify Thy name, nor can the bird of the human heart, however great its longing, ever hope to ascend into the heaven of Thy majesty and knowledge.

If I describe Thee, O my God, as Him Who is the All-Perceiving, I find myself compelled to admit that They Who are the highest Embodiments of perception have been created by virtue of Thy behest. And if I extol Thee as Him Who is the All-Wise, I, likewise, am forced to recognize that the Well Springs of wisdom have themselves been generated through the operation of Thy Will. And if I proclaim Thee as the Incomparable One, I soon discover that they Who are the inmost essence of oneness have been sent down by Thee and are but the evidences of Thine handiwork. And if I acclaim Thee as the Knower of all things, I must confess that they Who are the Quintessence of knowledge are but the creation and instruments of Thy Purpose.

Exalted, immeasurably exalted, art Thou above the strivings of mortal man to unravel Thy mystery, to describe Thy glory, or even to hint at the nature of Thine Essence. For whatever such strivings may accomplish, they never can hope to transcend the limitations imposed upon Thy creatures, inasmuch as these efforts are actuated by Thy decree, and are begotten of Thine invention. The loftiest sentiments which the holiest of saints can express in praise of Thee, and the deepest wisdom which the most learned of men can utter in their attempts to comprehend Thy nature, all revolve around that Centre Which is wholly subjected to Thy sovereignty, Which adoreth Thy Beauty, and is propelled through the movement of Thy Pen.

Nay, forbid it, O my God, that I should have uttered such words as must of necessity imply the existence of any direct relationship between the Pen of Thy Revelation and the essence of all created things. Far, far are They Who are related to Thee above the conception of such relationship! All comparisons and likenesses fail to do justice to the Tree of Thy Revelation, and every way is barred to the comprehension of the Manifestation of Thy Self and the Day Spring of Thy Beauty.

Far, far from Thy glory be what mortal man can affirm of Thee, or attribute unto Thee, or the praise with which he can glorify Thee! Whatever duty Thou hast prescribed unto Thy servants of extolling to the utmost Thy majesty and glory is but a token of Thy grace unto them, that they may be enabled to ascend unto the station conferred upon their own inmost being, the station of the knowledge of their own selves.

No one else besides Thee hath, at any time, been able to fathom Thy mystery, or befittingly to extol Thy greatness. Unsearchable and high above the praise of men wilt Thou remain for ever. There is none other God but Thee, the Inaccessible, the Omnipotent, the Omniscient, the Holy of Holies. [34]

Magnified be Thy name, O Lord My God! I know not what the water is with which Thou hast created me, or what the fire Thou hast kindled within me, or the clay wherewith Thou hast kneaded me. The restlessness of every sea hath been stilled, but not the restlessness of this Ocean which moveth at the bidding of the winds of Thy will. The flame of every fire hath been extinguished except the Flame which the hands of Thine omnipotence have kindled, and whose radiance Thou hast, by the power of Thy name, shed abroad before all that are in Thy heaven and all that are on Thy earth. As the tribulations deepen, it waxeth hotter and hotter.

Behold, then, O my God, how Thy Light hath been compassed with the onrushing winds of Thy decree, how the tempests that blow and beat upon it from every side have added to its brightness and increased its splendour. For all this let Thee be praised.

I implore Thee, by Thy Most Great Name, and Thy most ancient sovereignty, to look upon Thy loved ones whose hearts have been sorely shaken by reason of the troubles that have touched Him Who is the Manifestation of Thine own Self. Powerful art Thou to do what pleaseth Thee. Thou art, verily, the All-Knowing, the All-Wise. [35]

The hearts that yearn after Thee, O my God, are burnt up with the fire of their longing for Thee, and the eyes of them that love Thee weep sore by reason of their crushing separation from Thy court, and the voice of the lamentation of such as have set their hopes on Thee hath gone forth throughout Thy dominions.

Thou hast Thyself, O my God, protected them, by Thy sovereign might, from both extremities. But for the burning of their souls and the sighing of their hearts, they would be drowned in the midst of their tears, and but for the flood of their tears they would be burnt up by the fire of their hearts and the heat of their souls. Methinks, they are like the angels which Thou hast created of snow and of fire. Wilt Thou, despite such vehement longing, O my God, debar them from Thy presence, or drive them away, notwithstanding such fervour, from the door of Thy mercy? All hope is ready to be extinguished in the hearts of Thy chosen ones, O my God! Where are the breezes of Thy grace? They are hemmed in on all sides by their enemies; where are the ensigns of Thy triumph which Thou didst promise in Thy Tablets?

Thy glory is my witness! At each daybreak they who love Thee wake to find the cup of woe set before their faces, because they have believed in Thee and acknowledged Thy signs. Though I firmly believe that Thou hast a greater compassion on them than they have on their own selves, though I recognize that Thou hast afflicted them for no other purpose except to proclaim Thy Cause, and to enable them to ascend into the heaven of Thine eternity and the precincts of Thy court, yet Thou knowest full well the frailty of some of them, and art aware of their impatience in their sufferings.

Help them through Thy strengthening grace, I beseech Thee, O my God, to suffer patiently in their love for Thee, and unveil to their eyes what Thou hast decreed for them behind the Tabernacle of Thine unfailing protection, so that they may rush forward to meet what is preordained for them in Thy path, and may vie in hasting after tribulation in their love towards Thee. And if not, do Thou, then, reveal the standards of Thine ascendancy, and make them to be victorious over Thine adversaries, that Thy sovereignty may be manifested unto all the dwellers of Thy realm, and the power of Thy might demonstrated amidst Thy creatures. Powerful art Thou to do what Thou willest. No God is there but Thee, the Omniscient, the All-Wise.

Make steadfast Thou, O my God, Thy servant who hath believed in Thee to help Thy Cause, and keep him safe from all dangers in the stronghold of Thy care and Thy protection, both in this life and in the life which is to come. Thou, verily, rulest as Thou pleasest. No God is there save Thee, the Ever-Forgiving, the Most Generous.[36]

II   'Abdu'l-Bahá

From Paris Talks

THE DUTY OF KINDNESS AND SYMPATHY
TOWARDS STRANGERS AND FOREIGNERS

October 16th and 17th, 1911

When a man turns his face to God he finds sunshine everywhere. All men are his brothers. Let not conventionality cause you to seem cold and unsympathetic when you meet strange people from other countries . . .

Let those who meet you know, without your proclaiming the fact, that you are indeed a Bahá'í.

Put into practice the Teaching of Bahá'u'lláh, that of kindness to all nations. Do not be content with showing friendship in words alone, let your heart burn with loving kindness for all who may cross your path . . .

What profit is there in agreeing that universal friendship is good, and talking of the solidarity of the human race as a grand ideal? Unless these thoughts are translated into the world of action, they are useless.

The wrong in the world continues to exist just because people talk only of their ideals, and do not strive to put them into practice. If actions took the place of words, the world's misery would very soon be changed into comfort.

A man who does great good, and talks not of it, is on the way to perfection.

The man who has accomplished a small good and magnifies it in his speech is worth very little.

If I love you, I need not continually speak of my love – you will know without any words. On the other hand if I love you not, that also will you know – and you would not believe me, were I to tell you in a thousand words, that I loved you.

People make much profession of goodness, multiplying fine words because they wish to be thought greater and better than their fellows, seeking fame in the eyes of the world. Those who do most good use fewest words concerning their actions.

The children of God do the works without boasting, obeying His laws.

My hope for you is that you will ever avoid tyranny and oppression; that you will work without ceasing till justice reigns in every land, that you will keep your hearts pure and your hands free from unrighteousness.

This is what the near approach to God requires from you, and this is what I expect of you.

GOOD IDEAS MUST BE CARRIED INTO ACTION

November 8th, 1911

All over the world one hears beautiful sayings extolled and noble precepts admired. All men say they love what is good, and hate everything that is evil! Sincerity is to be admired, whilst lying is despicable. Faith is a virtue, and treachery is a disgrace to humanity. It is a blessed thing to gladden the hearts of men, and wrong to be the cause of pain. To be kind and merciful is right, while to hate is sinful. Justice is a noble quality and injustice an iniquity. That it is one's duty to be pitiful and harm no one, and to avoid jealousy and malice at all costs. Wisdom is the glory of man, not ignorance; light, not darkness! It is a good thing to turn one's face toward God, and foolishness to ignore Him. That it is our duty to guide man upward, and not to mislead him and be the cause of his downfall. There are many more examples like unto these.

But all these sayings are but words and we see very few of them carried into the world of action. On the contrary, we perceive that men are carried away by passion and selfishness, each man thinking only of what will benefit himself even if it means the ruin of his brother. They are all anxious to make their fortune and care little or nothing for the welfare of others. They are concerned about their *own* peace and comfort, while the condition of their fellows troubles them not at all.

Unhappily this is the road most men tread.

But Bahá'ís must not be thus; they must rise above this condition. Actions must be more to them than words. By their actions they must be merciful and not merely by their words. They must on all occasions confirm by their actions what they proclaim in words. Their deeds must prove their fidelity, and their actions must show forth Divine light.

Let your actions cry aloud to the world that you are indeed Bahá'ís, for it is *actions* that speak to the world and are the cause of the progress of humanity.

If we are true Bahá'ís speech is not needed. Our actions will help on the world, will spread civilization, will help the progress of science, and cause the arts to develop. Without action nothing in the material world can be accomplished, neither can words unaided advance a man in the spiritual Kingdom. It is not through lip-service only that the elect of God have attained to holiness, but by patient lives of active service they have brought light into the world.

Therefore strive that your actions day by day may be beautiful prayers. Turn towards God, and seek always to do that which is right and noble. Enrich the poor, raise the fallen, comfort the sorrowful, bring healing to the sick, reassure the fearful, rescue the oppressed, bring hope to the hopeless, shelter the destitute!

This is the work of a true Bahá'í, and this is what is expected of him. If we strive to do all this, then are we true Bahá'ís, but if we neglect it, we are not followers of the Light, and we have no right to the name.

God, who sees all hearts, knows how far our lives are the fulfilment of our words.

November 26th, 1911

I am deeply touched by the sympathetic words which have been addressed to me, and I hope that day by day true love and affection may grow among us. God has willed that love should be a vital force in the world, and you all know how I rejoice to speak of love.

All down the ages the prophets of God have been sent into the world to serve the cause of truth — Moses brought the law of truth, and all the prophets of Israel after him sought to spread it.

When Jesus came He lighted the flaming torch of truth, and carried it aloft so that the whole world might be illumined thereby. After Him came His chosen apostles, and they went far and wide, carrying the light of their Master's teaching into a dark world — and, in their turn, passed on.

Then came Muhammad, who in His time and way spread the knowledge of truth among a savage people; for this has always been the mission of God's elect.

So, at last, when Bahá'u'lláh arose in Persia, this was His most ardent desire, to rekindle the waning light of truth in all lands. All the holy ones of God have tried with heart and soul to spread the light of love and unity throughout the world, so that the darkness of materiality might disappear and the light of spirituality might shine forth among the children of men. Then would hate, slander and murder disappear, and in their stead love, unity and peace would reign.

All the Manifestations of God came with the same purpose, and they have all sought to lead men into the paths of virtue. Yet we, their servants, still dispute among ourselves! Why is it thus? Why do we not love one another and live in unity?

It is because we have shut our eyes to the underlying principle of all religions, that God is one, that He is the Father of us all, that we are all immersed in the ocean of His mercy and sheltered and protected by His loving care.

The glorious Sun of Truth shines for all alike, the waters of Divine Mercy immerse each one, and His Divine favour is bestowed on all His children.

This loving God desires peace for all His creatures — why, then, do they spend their time in war?

He loves and protects all His children — why do they forget Him?

He bestows His Fatherly care on us all — why do we neglect our brothers?

Surely, when we realize how God loves and cares for us, we should so order our lives that we may become more like Him.

God has created us, one and all — why do we act in opposition to His wishes, when we are all His children, and love the same Father? All these divisions we see on all sides, all these disputes and opposition, are caused because men cling to *ritual* and outward observances, and forget the simple, underlying truth. It is the *outward practices* of religion that are so different, and it is they that cause disputes and enmity — while the *reality* is always the same, and one. The Reality is the Truth, and truth has no division. Truth is God's guidance, it is the light of the world, it is love, it is mercy. These attributes of truth are also human virtues inspired by the Holy Spirit.

So let us one and all hold fast to truth, and we shall be free indeed!

The day is coming when all the religions of the world will unite, for in principle they are one already. There is no need for division, seeing that it is only the outward forms that separate them. Among the sons of men some souls are suffering through ignorance, let us hasten to teach them; others are like children needing care and education until they are grown, and some are sick — to these we must carry Divine healing.

Whether ignorant, childish or sick, they must be loved and helped, and not disliked because of their imperfection.

Doctors of religion were instituted to bring spiritual healing to the peoples and to be the cause of unity among the nations. If they become the cause of division they had better not exist! A remedy is given to cure a disease, but if it only succeeds in aggravating the complaint, it is better to leave it alone. If religion is only to be a cause of disunion it had better not exist.

All the Divine Manifestations sent by God into the world would have gone through their terrible hardships and sufferings for the single hope of spreading Truth, unity and concord among men. Christ endured a life of sorrow, pain and grief, to bring a perfect example of love into the world — and in spite of this we continue to act in a contrary spirit one towards the other!

Love is the fundamental principle of God's purpose for man, and He has commanded us to love each other even as He loves us. All these discords and disputes which we hear on all sides only tend to increase materiality.

The world for the most part is sunk in materialism, and the blessings of the Holy Spirit are ignored. There is so little real spiritual feeling, and the progress of the world is for the most part merely material. Men are becoming like unto beasts that perish, for we know that they have no spiritual feeling – they do not turn to God, they have no religion! These things belong to man alone, and if he is without them he is a prisoner of nature, and no whit better than an animal.

How can man be content to lead only an animal existence when God has made him so high a creature? . . .

I beseech you, one and all, to add your prayers to mine to the end that war and bloodshed may cease, and that love, friendship, peace and unity may reign in the world.

All down the ages we see how blood has stained the surface of the earth; but now a ray of greater light has come, man's intelligence is greater, spirituality is beginning to grow, and a time is *surely* coming when the religions of the world will be at peace. Let us leave the discordant arguments concerning outward forms, and let us join together to hasten forward the Divine Cause of unity, until all humanity knows itself to be one family, joined together in love.[37]

From The Promulgation of Universal Peace

RELIGION IS PROGRESSIVE

Religion is the outer expression of the divine reality. Therefore it must be living, vitalized, moving and progressive. If it be without motion and non-progressive it is without the divine life; it is dead. The divine institutes are continuously active and evolutionary; therefore the revelation of them must be progressive and continuous. All things are subject to re-formation. This is a century of life and renewal. Sciences and arts, industry and invention have been reformed. Law and ethics have been reconstituted, reorganized. The world of thought has been regenerated. Sciences of former ages and philosophies of the past are useless today. Present exigencies demand new methods of solution; world problems are without precedent. Old ideas and modes of thoughts are fast becoming obsolete. Ancient laws and archaic ethical systems will not meet the requirements of modern conditions, for this is clearly the century of a new life, the century of the revelation of the reality and therefore the greatest of all centuries. Consider how the scientific developments of fifty years have surpassed and eclipsed the knowledge and achievements of all the former ages combined. Would the announcements and theories of ancient astronomers explain our present knowledge of the sun-worlds and planetary systems? Would the mask of obscurity which beclouded mediaeval centuries meet the demand for clear-eyed vision and understanding which characterizes the world today? Will the despotism of former governments answer the call for freedom which has risen from the heart of humanity in this cycle of illumination? It is evident that no vital results are now forthcoming from the customs, institutions and standpoints of the past. In view of this, shall blind imitations of ancestral forms and theological interpretations continue to guide and control the religious life and spiritual development of humanity today? Shall man, gifted with the power of reason, unthinkingly follow and adhere to dogma, creeds and hereditary beliefs which will not bear the analysis of reason in this century of effulgent reality? Unquestionably this will not satisfy men of science, for when they find premise or conclusion contrary to present standards of proof and without real foundation, they reject that which has been formerly accepted as standard and correct and move forward from new foundations.

The divine prophets have revealed and founded religion. They have laid down certain laws and heavenly principles for the guidance of mankind. They have taught and promulgated the knowledge of God, established praiseworthy ethical ideals and inculcated the highest standards of virtues in the human world. Gradually these heavenly teachings and foundations of reality have been beclouded by human interpretations and dogmatic imitations of ancestral beliefs. The essential realities which the prophets laboured so hard to establish in human hearts and minds while undergoing ordeals and suffering tortures of persecution, have now well nigh vanished. Some of these heavenly messengers have been killed, some imprisoned; all of them despised and rejected while proclaiming the reality of divinity. Soon after their departure from this world, the essential truth of their teachings was lost sight of and dogmatic imitations adhered to.

Inasmuch as human interpretations and blind imitations differ widely, religious strife and disagreement have arisen among mankind, the light of true religion has been extinguished and the unity of the world of humanity destroyed. The prophets of God voiced the spirit of unity and agreement. They have been the founders of divine reality. Therefore if the nations of the world forsake imitations and investigate the reality underlying the revealed Word of God they will agree and become reconciled. For reality is one and not multiple.

The nations and religions are steeped in blind and bigoted imitations. A man is a Jew because his father was a Jew. The Muḥammadan follows implicitly the footsteps of his ancestors in belief and observance. The Buddhist is true to his heredity as a Buddhist. That is to say they profess religious belief blindly and without investigation, making unity and agreement impossible. It is evident therefore that this condition will not be remedied without a reformation in the world of religion. In other words the fundamental reality of the divine religions must be renewed, reformed, revoiced to mankind.

From the seed of reality, religion has grown into a tree which has put forth leaves and branches, blossoms and fruit. After a time this tree has fallen into a condition of decay. The leaves and blossoms have withered and perished; the tree has become stricken and fruitless. It is not reasonable that man should hold to the old tree, claiming that its life forces are undiminished, its fruit unequalled, its existence eternal. The seed of reality must be sown again in human hearts in order that a new tree may grow therefrom and new divine fruits refresh the world. By this means the nations and peoples now divergent in religion will be brought into unity, imitations will be forsaken and a universal brotherhood in the reality itself will be established. Warfare and strife will cease among mankind; all will be reconciled as servants of God. For all are sheltered beneath the tree of His providence and mercy. God is kind to all; He is the giver of bounty to all alike, even as His Holiness Jesus Christ has declared that God 'sendeth rain on the just and on the unjust'; that is to say, the mercy of God is universal. All humanity is under the protection of His love and favour, and unto all He has pointed the way of guidance and progress.

Progress is of two kinds, material and spiritual. The former is attained through observation of the surrounding existence and constitutes the foundation of civilization. Spiritual progress is through the breaths of the Holy Spirit and is the awakening of the conscious soul of man to perceive the reality of divinity. Material progress insures the happiness of the human world. Spiritual progress insures the happiness and eternal continuance of the soul. The prophets of God have founded the laws of divine civilization. They have been the root and fundamental source of all knowledge. They have established the principles of human brotherhood or fraternity which is of various kinds, such as the fraternity of family, of race, of nation and of ethical motives. These forms of fraternity, these bonds of brotherhood are merely temporal and transient in association. They do not ensure harmony and are usually productive of disagreement. They do not prevent warfare and strife; on the contrary they are selfish, restricted and fruitful causes of enmity and hatred among mankind. The spiritual brotherhood which is enkindled and established through the breaths of the Holy Spirit unites nations and removes the cause of warfare and strife. It transforms mankind into one great family and establishes the foundation of the oneness of humanity. It promulgates the spirit of international agreement and insures Universal Peace. Therefore we must investigate the foundation reality of this heavenly fraternity. We must forsake all imitations and promote the reality of the divine teachings. In accordance with these principles and actions and by the assistance of the Holy Spirit, both material and spiritual happiness shall become realized. Until all nations and peoples become united by the bonds of the Holy Spirit in this real fraternity, until national and international prejudices are effaced in the reality of this spiritual brotherhood, true progress, prosperity and lasting happiness will not be attained by man. This is the century of new and universal nationhood. Sciences have advanced, industries have progressed, politics have been reformed, liberty has been proclaimed, justice is awakening. This is the century of motion, divine stimulus and accomplishment; the century of human solidarity and altruistic service; the century of Universal Peace and the reality of the divine kingdom.[38]

ON THE EQUALITY OF THE SEXES

Today questions of the utmost importance are facing humanity, questions peculiar to this radiant century. In former centuries there was not even mention of them. Inasmuch as this is the century of illumination, the century of humanity, the century of divine bestowals, these questions are being presented for the expression of public opinion, and in all the countries of the world, discussion is taking place looking to their solution.

One of these questions concerns the rights of woman and her equality with man. In past ages it was held that woman and man were not equal – that is to say, woman was considered inferior to man, even from the standpoint of her anatomy and creation. She was considered especially inferior in intelligence, and the idea prevailed universally that it was not allowable for her to step into the arena of important affairs. In some countries man went so far as to believe and teach that woman belonged to a sphere lower than human. But in this century, which is the century of light and the revelation of mysteries, God is proving to the satisfaction of humanity that all this is ignorance and error; nay, rather, it is well established that mankind and womankind as parts of composite humanity are coequal and that no difference in estimate is allowable, for all are human. The conditions in past centuries were due to woman's lack of opportunity. She was denied the right and privilege of education and left in her undeveloped state. Naturally, she could not and did not advance. In reality, God has created all mankind, and in the estimation of God there is no distinction as to male and female. The one whose heart is pure is acceptable in His sight, be that one man or woman. God does not inquire, 'Art thou woman or art thou man?' He judges human actions. If these are acceptable in the threshold of the Glorious One, man and woman will be equally recognized and rewarded.

Furthermore, the education of woman is more necessary and important than that of man, for woman is the trainer of the child from its infancy. If she be defective and imperfect herself, the child will necessarily be deficient; therefore, imperfection of woman implies a condition of imperfection in all mankind, for it is the mother who rears, nurtures and guides the growth of the child. This is not the function of the father. If the educator be incompetent, the educated will be correspondingly lacking. This is evident and incontrovertible. Could the student be brilliant and accomplished if the teacher is illiterate and ignorant? The mothers are the first educators of mankind; if they be imperfect, alas for the condition and future of the race.

Again, it is well established in history that where woman has not participated in human affairs the outcomes have never attained a state of completion and perfection. On the other hand, every influential undertaking of the human world wherein woman has been a participant has attained importance. This is historically true and beyond disproof even in religion. Jesus Christ had twelve disciples and among His followers a woman known as Mary Magdalene. Judas Iscariot had become a traitor and hypocrite, and after the crucifixion the remaining eleven disciples were wavering and undecided. It is certain from the evidence of the Gospels that the one who comforted them and reestablished their faith was Mary Magdalene.

The world of humanity consists of two parts: male and female. Each is the complement of the other. Therefore, if one is defective, the other will necessarily be incomplete, and perfection cannot be attained. There is a right hand and a left hand in the human body, functionally equal in service and administration. If either proves defective, the defect will naturally extend to the other by involving the completeness of the whole; for accomplishment is not normal unless both are perfect. If we say one hand is deficient, we prove the inability and incapacity of the other; for single-handed there is no full accomplishment. Just as physical accomplishment is complete with two hands, so man and woman, the two parts of the social body, must be perfect. It is not natural that either should remain undeveloped; and until both are perfected, the happiness of the human world will not be realized.

The most momentous question of this day is international peace and arbitration, and universal peace is impossible without universal suffrage. Children are educated by the women. The mother bears the troubles and anxieties of rearing the child, undergoes the ordeal of its birth and training. Therefore, it is most difficult for mothers to send to the battlefield those upon whom they have lavished such love and care. Consider a son reared and trained twenty years by a devoted mother. What sleepless nights and restless, anxious days she has spent! Having brought him through dangers and difficulties to the age of maturity, how agonizing then to sacrifice him upon the battlefield! Therefore, the mothers will not sanction war nor be satisfied with it. So it will come to pass that when women participate fully and equally in the affairs of the world, when they enter confidently and capably the great arena of laws and politics, war will cease; for woman will be the obstacle and hindrance to it. This is true and without doubt.

It has been objected by some that woman is not equally capable with man and that she is deficient by creation. This is pure imagination. The difference in capability between man and woman is due entirely to opportunity and education. Heretofore woman has been denied the right and privilege of equal development. If equal opportunity be granted her, there is no doubt she would be the peer of man. History will evidence this. In past ages noted women have arisen in the affairs of nations and surpassed men in their accomplishments . . .

The purpose, in brief, is this: that if woman be fully educated and granted her rights, she will attain the capacity for wonderful accomplishments and prove herself the equal of man. She is the coadjutor of man, his complement and helpmeet. Both are human; both are endowed with potentialities of intelligence and embody the virtues of humanity. In all human powers and functions they are partners and coequals. At present in spheres of human activity woman does not manifest her natal prerogatives, owing to lack of education and opportunity. Without doubt education will establish her equality with men. Consider the animal kingdom, where no distinction is observed between male and female. They are equal in powers and privileges. Among birds of the air no distinction is evidenced. Their powers are equal; they dwell together in complete unity and mutual recognition of rights. Shall we not enjoy the same equality? Its absence is not befitting to mankind. 39

From The Tablet to the Hague (a letter written to the Central Organization for a Durable Peace, December 17th, 1919)

O ye esteemed ones who are pioneers among the well-wishers of the world of humanity!

The letters which ye sent during the war were not received, but a letter dated 11 February 1916, has just come to hand, and immediately an answer is being written. Your intention deserves a thousand praises, because you are serving the world of humanity, and this is conducive to the happiness and welfare of all. This recent war has proved to the world and the people that war is destruction while Universal Peace is construction; war is death while peace is life . . .

There is not one soul whose conscience does not testify that in this day there is no more important matter in the world than that of Universal Peace. Every just one bears witness to this and adores that esteemed Assembly because its aim is that this darkness may be changed into light . . .

But the wise souls who are aware of the essential relationships emanating from the realities of things consider that one single matter cannot, by itself, influence the human reality as it ought and should, for until the minds of men become united, no important matter can be accomplished. At present Universal Peace is a matter of great importance, but unity of conscience is essential, so that the foundation of this matter may become secure, its establishment firm and its edifice strong.

Therefore His Holiness Bahá'u'lláh, fifty years ago, expounded this question of Universal Peace at a time when he was confined in the fortress of 'Akká and was wronged and imprisoned. He wrote about this important matter of Universal Peace to all the great sovereigns of the world, and established it among his friends in the Orient. The horizon of the East was in utter darkness, nations displayed the utmost hatred and enmity towards each other, religions thirsted for each other's blood, and it was darkness upon darkness. At such a time His Holiness Bahá'u'lláh shone forth like the sun from the horizon of the East and illumined Persia with the lights of these teachings.

Among his teachings was the declaration of Universal Peace. People of different nations, religions and sects who followed him came together to such an extent that remarkable gatherings were instituted consisting of the various nations and religions of the East. Every soul who entered these gatherings saw but one nation, one teaching, one pathway, one order, for the teachings of His Holiness Bahá'u'lláh were not limited to the establishment of Universal Peace. They embraced many teachings which supplemented and supported that of Universal Peace.

Among these teachings was the independent investigation of reality so that the world of humanity may be saved from the darkness of imitation and attain to the truth; may tear off and cast away this ragged and outgrown garment of 1,000 years ago and may put on the robe woven in the utmost purity and holiness in the loom of reality. As reality is one and cannot admit of multiplicity, therefore different opinions must ultimately become fused into one.

And among the teachings of His Holiness Bahá'u'lláh is the oneness of the world of humanity; that all human beings are the sheep of God and He is the kind Shepherd. This Shepherd is kind to all the sheep, because He created them all, trained them, provided for them and protected them . . .

And among the teachings of His Holiness Bahá'u'lláh is, that religion must be the cause of fellowship and love. If it becomes the cause of estrangement then it is not needed, for religion is like a remedy; if it aggravates the disease then it becomes unnecessary.

And among the teachings of Bahá'u'lláh is, that religion must be in conformity with science and reason, so that it may influence the hearts of men. The foundation must be solid and must not consist of imitations.

And among the teachings of Bahá'u'lláh is, that religious, racial, political, economic and patriotic prejudices destroy the edifice of humanity. As long as these prejudices prevail, the world of humanity will not have rest. For a period of 6,000 years history informs us about the world of humanity. During these 6,000 years the world of humanity has not been free from war, strife, murder and bloodthirstiness. In every period war has been waged in one country or another and that war was due to either religious prejudice, racial prejudice, political prejudice or patriotic prejudice . . . As long as these prejudices persist, the struggle for existence must remain dominant, and bloodthirstiness and rapacity continue. Therefore, even as was the case in the past, the world of humanity cannot be saved from the darkness of nature and cannot attain illumination except through the abandonment of prejudices and the acquisition of the morals of the Kingdom.

If this prejudice and enmity are on account of religion (consider that) religion should be the cause of fellowship, otherwise it is fruitless. And if this prejudice be the prejudice of nationality (consider that) all mankind are of one nation; all have sprung from the tree of Adam, and Adam is the root of the tree. That tree is one and all these nations are like branches, while the individuals of humanity are like leaves, blossoms and fruits thereof. Then the establishment of various nations and the consequent shedding of blood and destruction of the edifice of humanity result from human ignorance and selfish motives.

As to the patriotic prejudice, this is also due to absolute ignorance, for the surface of the earth is one native land. Every one can live in any spot on the terrestrial globe. Therefore all the world is man's birthplace. These boundaries and outlets have been devised by man. In the creation, such boundaries and outlets were not assigned . . . God has set up no frontier between France and Germany; they are continuous. Yea, in the first centuries, selfish souls, for the promotion of their own interests, have assigned boundaries and outlets and have, day by day, attached more importance to these, until this led to intense enmity, bloodshed and rapacity in subsequent centuries. In the same way this will continue indefinitely, and if this conception of patriotism remains limited within a certain circle, it will be the primary cause of the world's destruction. No wise and just person will acknowledge these imaginary distinctions. Every limited area which we call our native country we regard as our mother-land, whereas the terrestrial globe is the mother-land of all, and not any restricted area. In short, for a few days we live on this earth and eventually we are buried in it, it is our eternal tomb. Is it worth while that we should engage in bloodshed and tear one another to pieces for this eternal tomb? Nay, far from it, neither is God pleased with such conduct nor would any sane man approve of it.

Consider! The blessed animals engage in no patriotic quarrels. They are in the utmost fellowship with one another and live together in harmony. For example, if a dove from the East and a dove from the West, a dove from the North and a dove from the South chance to arrive, at the same time, in one spot, they immediately associate in harmony. So is it with all the blessed animals and birds. But the ferocious animals, as soon as they meet, attack and fight with each other, tear each other to pieces and it is impossible for them to live peaceably together in one spot. They are all unsociable and fierce, savage and combative fighters.

Regarding the economic prejudice, it is apparent that whenever the ties between nations become strengthened and the exchange of commodities accelerated, and any economic principle is established in one country, it will ultimately affect the other countries and universal benefits will result. Then why this prejudice? . . .

And among the teachings of His Holiness Bahá'u'lláh is the origination of one language that may be spread universally among the people. This teaching was revealed from the pen of His Holiness Bahá'u'lláh in order that this universal language may eliminate misunderstandings from among mankind.

And among the teachings of His Holiness Bahá'u'lláh is the equality of women and men. The world of humanity has two wings — one is women and the other men. Not until both wings are equally developed can the bird fly. Should one wing remain weak, flight is impossible. Not until the world of women becomes equal to the world of men in the acquisition of virtues and perfections, can success and prosperity be attained as they ought to be.

And among the teachings of Bahá'u'lláh is voluntary sharing of one's property with others among mankind. This voluntary sharing is greater than equality, and consists in this, that man should not prefer himself to others, but rather should sacrifice his life and property for others. But this should not be introduced by coercion so that it becomes a law and man is compelled to follow. Nay, rather, man should voluntarily and of his own choice sacrifice his property and life for others, and spend willingly for the poor, just as is done in Persia among the Bahá'ís.

And among the teachings of His Holiness Bahá'u'lláh is man's freedom, that through the ideal Power he should be free and emancipated from the captivity of the world of nature; for as long as man is captive to nature he is a ferocious animal, as the struggle for existence is one of the exigencies of the world of nature. This matter of the struggle for existence is the fountain-head of all calamities and is the supreme affliction.

And among the teachings of Bahá'u'lláh is that religion is a mighty bulwark. If the edifice of religion shakes and totters, commotion and chaos will ensue and the order of things will be utterly upset, for in the world of mankind there are two safeguards that protect man from wrong-doing. One is the law which punishes the criminal; but the law prevents only the manifest crime and not the concealed sin; whereas the ideal safeguard, namely, the religion of God, prevents both the manifest and the concealed crime, trains man, educates morals, compels the adoption of virtues and is the all-inclusive power which guarantees the felicity of the world of mankind. But by religion is meant that which is ascertained by investigation and not that which is based on mere imitation, the foundation of Divine Religions and not human imitations.

And among the teachings of Bahá'u'lláh is that although material civilization is one of the means for the progress of the world of mankind, yet until it becomes combined with Divine civilization, the desired result, which is the felicity of mankind, will not be attained. Consider! These battleships that reduce a city to ruins within the space of an hour are the result of material civilization; likewise the Krupp guns, the Mauser rifles, dynamite, submarines, torpedo boats, armed aircraft and bombing aeroplanes – all these weapons of war are the malignant fruits of material civilization. Had material civilization been combined with Divine civilization, these fiery weapons would never have been invented. Nay, rather, human energy would have been wholly devoted to useful inventions and would have been concentrated on praiseworthy discoveries. Material civilization is like a lamp-glass. Divine civilization is the lamp itself and the glass without the light is dark. Material civilization is like the body. No matter how infinitely graceful, elegant and beautiful it may be, it is dead. Divine civilization is like the spirit, and the body gets its life from the spirit, otherwise it becomes a corpse. It has thus been made evident that the world of mankind is in need of the breaths of the Holy Spirit. Without the spirit the world of mankind is lifeless, and without this light the world of mankind is in utter darkness. For the world of nature is an animal world. Until man is born again from the world of nature, that is to say, becomes detached from the world of nature, he is essentially an animal, and it is the teachings of God which convert this animal into a human soul.

And among the teachings of Bahá'u'lláh is the promotion of education. Every child must be instructed in sciences as much as is necessary. If the parents are able to provide the expenses of this education, it is all right, otherwise the community must provide the means for the teaching of that child.

And among the teachings of His Holiness Bahá'u'lláh is justice and right. Until these are realized on the plane of existence, all things shall be in disorder and remain imperfect. The world of mankind is a world of oppression and cruelty, and a realm of aggression and error.

In fine, such teachings are numerous. These manifold principles, which constitute the greatest basis for the felicity of mankind and are of the bounties of the Merciful, must be added to the matter of Universal Peace and combined with it, so that results may accrue. Otherwise the realization of Universal Peace (by itself) in the world of mankind is difficult. As the teachings of His Holiness Bahá'u'lláh are combined with Universal Peace, they are like a table provided with every kind of fresh and delicious food. Every soul can find, at that table of infinite bounty, that which he desires. If the question is restricted to Universal Peace alone, the remarkable results which are expected and desired will not be attained. The scope of Universal Peace must be such that all the communities and religions may find their highest wish realized in it. At present the teachings of His Holiness Bahá'u'lláh are such that all the communities of the world, whether religious, political or ethical, ancient or modern, find in the teachings of Bahá'u'lláh the expression of their highest wish.

For example, the people of religions find, in the teachings of His Holiness Bahá'u'lláh, the establishment of Universal Religion — a religion that perfectly conforms with present conditions, which in reality effects the immediate cure of the incurable disease, which relieves every pain, and bestows the infallible antidote for every deadly poison. For if we wish to arrange and organize the world of mankind in accordance with the present religious imitations and thereby to establish the felicity of the world of mankind, it is impossible and impracticable — for example, the enforcement of the laws of the Old Testament (Taurat) and also of the other religions in accordance with present imitations. But the essential basis of all the Divine Religions which pertains to the virtues of the world of mankind and is the foundation of the welfare of the world of man, is found in the teachings of His Holiness Bahá'u'lláh in the most perfect presentation.

Similarly, with regard to the peoples who clamour for freedom: the moderate freedom which guarantees the welfare of the world of mankind and maintains and preserves the universal relationships, is found in its fullest power and extension in the teachings of His Holiness Bahá'u'lláh.

So with regard to political parties: that which is the greatest policy directing the world of mankind, nay, rather, the Divine policy, is found in the teachings of His Holiness Bahá'u'lláh.

Likewise with regard to the party of 'equality' which seeks the solution of the economic problems: until now all proposed solutions have proved impracticable except the economic proposals in the teachings of His Holiness Bahá'u'lláh which are practicable and cause no distress to society.

So with the other parties: when ye look deeply into this matter, ye will discover that the highest aims of those parties are found in the teachings of Bahá'u'lláh. These teachings constitute the all-inclusive power among all men and are practicable. But there are some teachings of the past, such as those of the Taurat, which cannot be carried out at the present day. It is the same with the other religions and the tenets of the various sects and the different parties.

For example, the question of Universal Peace, about which His Holiness Bahá'u'lláh says that the Supreme Tribunal must be established: although the League of Nations has been brought into existence, yet it is incapable of establishing Universal Peace. But the Supreme Tribunal which His Holiness Bahá'u'lláh has described will fulfil this sacred task with the utmost might and power. And His plan is this: that the national assemblies of each country and nation – that is to say parliaments – should elect two or three persons who are the choicest men of that nation, and are well informed concerning international laws and the relations between governments and aware of the essential needs of the world of humanity of this day. The number of these representatives should be in proportion to the number of inhabitants of that country. The election of these souls who are chosen by the national assembly, that is, the parliament, must be confirmed by the upper house, the congress and the cabinet and also by the president or monarch so these persons may be the elected ones of all the nation and the government. From among these people the members of the Supreme Tribunal will be elected, and all mankind will thus have a share therein, for every one of these delegates is fully representative of his nation. When the Supreme Tribunal gives a ruling on any international question, either unanimously or by majority-rule, there will no longer be any pretext for the plaintiff or ground of objection for the defendant. In case any of the governments or nations in the execution of the irrefutable decision of the Supreme Tribunal, be negligent or dilatory, the rest of the nations will rise up against it, because all the governments and nations of the world are the supporters of this Supreme Tribunal. Consider what a firm foundation this is! But by a limited and restricted *League* the purpose will not be realized as it ought and should. This is the truth about the situation, which has been stated.

Consider how powerful are the teachings of His Holiness Bahá'u'lláh. At a time when His Holiness was in the prison of 'Akká and was under the restrictions and threats of two bloodthirsty kings, notwithstanding this fact, His teachings spread with all power in Persia and other countries. Should any teaching, or any principle, or any community fall under the threat of a powerful and bloodthirsty monarch it will be annihilated within a short space of time. At present for fifty years the Bahá'ís in Persia and most regions have been under severe restrictions and the threat of sword and spear. Thousands of souls have given their lives in the arena of sacrifice and have fallen as victims under the swords of oppression and cruelty. Thousands of esteemed families have been uprooted and destroyed. Thousands of children have been made fatherless. Thousands of fathers have been bereft of their sons. Thousands of mothers have wept and lamented for their boys who have been beheaded. All this oppression and cruelty, rapacity and bloodthirstiness did not hinder or prevent the spread of the teachings of Bahá'u'lláh. They spread more and more every day, and their power and might became more evident . . .

In fine, when travelling and journeying throughout the world, wherever one finds construction, it is the result of fellowship and love, while everything that is in ruin shows the effect of enmity and hatred. Notwithstanding this, the world of humanity has not become aware and has not awakened from the sleep of heedlessness. Again it engages in differences, in disputes and wrangling, that it may set up ranks of war and may run to and fro in the arena of battle and strife.

So is it with regard to the universe and its corruption, existence and non-existence. Every contingent being is made up of different and numerous elements and the existence of everything is a result of composition. That is to say, when between simple elements a composition takes place a being arises; the creation of beings come about in this way. And when that composition is upset, it is followed by decomposition, the elements disintegrate, and that being becomes annihilated. That is to say, the annihilation of everything consists in the decomposition and the separation of elements. Therefore every union and colour of leaves, of flowers and of fruits, each will contribute to the beauty and charm of the others and will make an admirable garden, and will appear in the utmost loveliness, freshness and sweetness. Likewise, when difference and variety of thoughts, forms, opinions, characters and morals of the world of mankind come under the control of one Supreme Power, that influence of composition among the elements is the cause of life, while dissociation and separation is the cause of death. In short, attraction and harmony of things are the cause of the production of fruits and useful results, while repulsion and inharmony of things are the cause of disturbance and annihilation. From harmony and attraction, all living contingent beings, such as plant, animal and man, are realized, and from inharmony and repulsion decay sets in and annihilation becomes manifest. Therefore whatever is the cause of harmony, attraction and union among men is the life of the world of humanity, and whatever is the cause of difference, of repulsion and of separation is the cause of the death of mankind. And when you pass by a garden wherein vegetable beds and plants, flowers and fragrant herbs are all combined so as to form a harmonious whole, this is an evidence that this plantation and this rose garden have been cultivated and arranged by the care of a perfect gardener, while when you see a garden in disorder, lacking arrangement and confused, this indicates that it has been deprived of the care of a skilful gardener, nay, rather it is nothing but a mass of weeds. It has therefore been made evident that fellowship and harmony are indicative of the training by the real Educator, while separation and dispersion prove wildness and deprivation of Divine training.

Should any one object that, since the communities and nations and races and peoples of the world have different formalities, customs, tastes, temperaments, morals, varied thoughts, minds and opinions, it is therefore impossible for ideal unity to be made manifest and complete union among men to be realized, we say that differences are of two kinds: One leads to destruction, and that is like the difference between warring peoples and competing nations who destroy one another, uproot each other's families, do away with rest and comfort and engage in bloodshed and rapacity. That is blameworthy. But the other difference consists in variation. This is perfection itself and the cause of the appearance of Divine bounty. Consider the flowers of the rose garden. Although they are of different kinds, various colours and diverse forms and appearances, yet as they drink from one water, are swayed by one breeze and grow by the warmth and light of one sun, this variation and this difference cause each to enhance the beauty and splendour of the others. The differences in manners, in customs, in habits, in thoughts, opinions and in temperaments is the cause of the adornment of the world of mankind. This is praiseworthy. Likewise this difference and this variation, like the difference and variation of the parts and members of the human body, are the cause of the appearance of beauty and perfection. As these different parts and members are under the control of the dominant spirit, and the spirit permeates all the organs and members, and rules all the arteries and veins, this difference and this variation strengthen love and harmony and this multiplicity is the greatest aid to unity. If in a garden the flowers and fragrant herbs, the blossoms and fruits, the leaves, branches and trees are of one kind, of one form, of one colour and one arrangement, there is no beauty or sweetness, but when there is variety in the world of oneness, they will appear and be displayed in the most perfect glory, beauty, exaltation and perfection. Today nothing but the power of the Word of God which encompasses the realities of things can bring the thoughts, the minds, the hearts and the spirits under the shade of one Tree. He is the potent in all things, the vivifier of souls, the preserver and the controller of the world of mankind. Praise be to God, in this day the light of the Word of God has shone forth upon all regions, and from all sects, communities, nations, tribes, peoples, religions and denominations, souls have gathered under the shadow of the Word of Oneness and have in the most intimate fellowship united and harmonized![40]

III Shoghi Effendi

From The Unfoldment of World Civilization (letter to the Bahá'ís of the West, 11 March 1936)

Dearly-beloved friends: Though the Revelation of Bahá'u'lláh has been delivered, the World Order which such a Revelation must needs beget is as yet unborn. Though the Heroic Age of His Faith is passed, the creative energies which that Age has released have not as yet crystallized into that world society which, in the fullness of time, is to mirror forth the brightness of His glory. Though the framework of His Administrative Order has been erected, and the Formative Period of the Bahá'í Era has begun, yet the promised Kingdom into which the seed of His institutions must ripen remains as yet uninaugurated. Though His Voice has been raised, and the ensigns of His Faith have been lifted up in no less than forty countries of both the East and the West, yet the wholeness of the human race is as yet unrecognized, its unity unproclaimed, and the standard of its Most Great Peace unhoisted.

'The heights,' Bahá'u'lláh Himself testifies, 'which, through the most gracious favour of God, mortal man can attain in this Day are as yet unrevealed to his sight. The world of being hath never had, nor doth it yet possess, the capacity for such a revelation. The day, however, is approaching when the potentialities of so great a favour will, by virtue of His behest, be manifested unto men.'

For the revelation of so great a favour a period of intense turmoil and wide-spread suffering would seem to be indispensable. Resplendent as has been the Age that has witnessed the inception of the Mission with which Bahá'u'lláh has been entrusted, the interval which must elapse ere that Age yields its choicest fruit must, it is becoming increasingly apparent, be overshadowed by such moral and social gloom as can alone prepare an unrepentant humanity for the prize she is destined to inherit.

Into such a period we are now steadily and irresistibly moving. Amidst the shadows which are increasingly gathering about us we can faintly discern the glimmerings of Bahá'u'lláh's unearthly sovereignty appearing fitfully on the horizon of history. To us, the 'generation of the half-light', living at a time which may be designated as the period of the incubation of the World Commonwealth envisaged by Bahá'u'lláh, has been assigned a task whose high privilege we can never sufficiently appreciate, and the arduousness of which we can as yet but dimly recognize. We may well believe, we who are called upon to experience the operation of the dark forces destined to unloose a flood of agonizing afflictions, that the darkest hour that must precede the dawn of the Golden Age of our Faith has not yet struck. Deep as is the gloom that already encircles the world, the afflictive ordeals which that world is to suffer are still in preparation, nor can their blackness be as yet imagined. We stand on the threshold of an age whose convulsions proclaim alike the death-pangs of the old order and the birth-pangs of the new. Through the generating influence of the Faith announced by Bahá'u'lláh this New World Order may be said to have been conceived. We can, at the present moment, experience its stirrings in the womb of a travailing age — an age waiting for the appointed hour at which it can cast its burden and yield its fairest fruit.

'The whole earth', writes Bahá'u'lláh, 'is now in a state of pregnancy. The day is approaching when it will have yielded its noblest fruits, when from it will have sprung forth the loftiest trees, the most enchanting blossoms, the most heavenly blessings. Immeasurably exalted is the breeze that wafteth from the garment of thy Lord, the Glorified! For lo, it hath breathed its fragrance and made all things new! Well is it with them that comprehend . . .'

As we view the world around us, we are compelled to observe the manifold evidences of that universal fermentation which, in every continent of the globe and in every department of human life, be it religious, social, economic or political, is purging and reshaping humanity in anticipation of the Day when the wholeness of the human race will have been recognized and its unity established. A two-fold process, however, can be distinguished, each tending, in its own way and with an accelerated momentum, to bring to a climax the forces that are transforming the face of our planet. The first is essentially an integrating process, while the second is fundamentally disruptive. The former, as it steadily evolves, unfolds a System which may well serve as a pattern for that world polity towards which a strangely-disordered world is continually advancing; while the latter, as its disintegrating influence deepens, tends to tear down, with increasing violence, the antiquated barriers that seek to block humanity's progress towards its destined goal. The constructive process stands associated with the nascent Faith of Bahá'u'lláh, and is the harbinger of the New World Order that Faith must erelong establish. The destructive forces that characterize the other should be identified with a civilization that has refused to answer to the expectation of a new age, and is consequently falling into chaos and decline.

A titanic, a spiritual struggle, unparalleled in its magnitude yet unspeakably glorious in its ultimate consequences, is being waged as a result of these opposing tendencies, in this age of transition through which the organized community of the followers of Bahá'u'lláh and mankind as a whole are passing.

The Spirit that has incarnated itself in the institutions of a rising Faith has, in the course of its onward march for the redemption of the world, encountered and is now battling with such forces as are, in most instances, the very negation of that Spirit, and whose continued existence must inevitably hinder it from achieving its purpose. The hollow and outworn institutions, the obsolescent doctrines and beliefs, the effete and discredited traditions which these forces represent, it should be observed, have, in certain instances, been undermined by virtue of their senility, the loss of their cohesive power, and their own inherent corruption. A few have been swept away by the onrushing forces which the Bahá'í Faith has, at the hour of its birth, so mysteriously released. Others, as a direct result of a vain and feeble resistance to its rise in the initial stages of its development, have died out and been utterly discredited. Still others, fearful of the pervasive influence of the institutions in which that same Spirit had, at a later stage, been embodied, had mobilized their forces and launched their attack, destined to sustain, in their turn, after a brief and illusory success, an ignominious defeat. . . .

Beset on every side by the cumulative evidences of disintegration, of turmoil and of bankruptcy, serious-minded men and women, in almost every walk of life, are beginning to doubt whether society, as it is now organized, can, through its unaided efforts, extricate itself from the slough into which it is steadily sinking. Every system, short of the unification of the human race, has been tried, repeatedly tried, and been found wanting. Wars again and again have been fought, and conferences without number have met and deliberated. Treaties, pacts and covenants have been painstakingly negotiated, concluded and revised. Systems of government have been patiently tested, have been continually recast and superseded. Economic plans of reconstruction have been carefully devised, and meticulously executed. And yet crisis has succeeded crisis, and the rapidity with which a perilously unstable world is declining has been correspondingly accelerated. A yawning gulf threatens to involve in one common disaster both the satisfied and dissatisfied nations, democracies and dictatorships, capitalists and wage-earners, Europeans and Asiatics, Jew and Gentile, white and coloured. An angry Providence, the cynic might well observe, has abandoned a hapless planet to its fate, and fixed irrevocably its doom. Sore-tried and disillusioned, humanity has no doubt lost its orientation, and would seem to have lost as well its faith and hope. It is hovering, unshepherded and visionless, on the brink of disaster. A sense of fatality seems to pervade it. An ever-deepening gloom is settling on its fortunes as she recedes further and further from the outer fringes of the darkest zone of its agitated life and penetrates its very heart.

And yet while the shadows are continually deepening, might we not claim that gleams of hope, flashing intermittently on the international horizon, appear at times to relieve the darkness that encircles humanity? Would it be untrue to maintain that in a world of unsettled faith and disturbed thought, a world of steadily mounting armaments, of unquenchable hatreds and rivalries, the progress, however fitful, of the forces working in harmony with the spirit of the age can already be discerned? Though the great outcry raised by post-war nationalism is growing louder and more insistent every day, the League of Nations is as yet in its embryonic state, and the storm clouds that are gathering may for a time totally eclipse its powers and obliterate its machinery, yet the direction in which the institution itself is operating is most significant. The voices that have been raised ever since its inception, the efforts that have been exerted, the work that has already been accomplished, foreshadow the triumphs which this presently constituted institution, or any other body that may supersede it, is destined to achieve . . .

The long ages of infancy and childhood, through which the human race had to pass, have receded into the background. Humanity is now experiencing the commotions invariably associated with the most turbulent stage of its evolution, the stage of adolescence, when the impetuosity of youth and its vehemence reach their climax, and must gradually be superseded by the calmness, the wisdom, and the maturity that characterize the stage of manhood. Then will the human race reach that stature of ripeness which will enable it to acquire all the powers and capacities upon which its ultimate development must depend.

Unification of the whole of mankind is the hall-mark of the stage which human society is now approaching. Unity of family, of tribe, of city-state, and nation have been successively attempted and fully established. World unity is the goal towards which a harassed humanity is striving. Nation-building has come to an end. The anarchy inherent in state sovereignty is moving towards a climax. A world, growing to maturity, must abandon this fetish, recognize the oneness and wholeness of human relationships, and establish once for all the machinery that can best incarnate this fundamental principle of its life . . .

The unity of the human race, as envisaged by Bahá'u'lláh, implies the establishment of a world commonwealth in which all nations, races, creeds and classes are closely and permanently united, and in which the autonomy of its state members and the personal freedom and initiative of the individuals that compose them are definitely and completely safeguarded. This commonwealth must, as far as we can visualize it, consist of a world legislature, whose members will, as the trustees of the whole of mankind, ultimately control the entire resources of all the component nations, and will enact such laws as shall be required to regulate the life, satisfy the needs and adjust the relationships of all races and peoples. A world executive, backed by an international Force, will carry out the decisions arrived at, and apply the laws enacted by, this world legislature, and will safeguard the organic unity of the whole commonwealth. A world tribunal will adjudicate and deliver its compulsory and final verdict in all and any disputes that may arise between the various elements constituting this universal system. A mechanism of world inter-communication will be devised, embracing the whole planet, freed from national hindrances and restrictions, and functioning with marvellous swiftness and perfect regularity. A world metropolis will act as the nerve centre of a world civilization, the focus towards which the unifying forces of life will converge and from which its energizing influences will radiate A world language will either be invented or chosen from among the existing languages and will be taught in the schools of all the federated nations as an auxiliary to their mother tongue. A world script, a world literature, a uniform and universal system of currency, of weights and measures, will simplify and facilitate intercourse and understanding among the nations and races of mankind.

In such a world society, science and religion, the two most potent forces in human life, will be reconciled, will cooperate, and will harmoniously develop. The press will, under such a system, while giving full scope to the expression of the diversified views and convictions of mankind, cease to be mischievously manipulated by vested interests, whether private or public, and will be liberated from the influence of contending governments and peoples. The economic resources of the world will be organized, its sources of raw materials will be tapped and fully utilized, its markets will be coordinated and developed, and the distribution of its products will be equitably regulated.

National rivalries, hatreds, and intrigues will cease, and racial animosity and prejudice will be replaced by racial amity, understanding and cooperation. The causes of religious strife will be permanently removed, economic barriers and restrictions will be completely abolished, and the inordinate distinction between classes will be obliterated. Destitution on the one hand, and gross accumulation of ownership on the other, will disappear. The enormous energy dissipated and wasted on war, whether economic or political, will be consecrated to such ends as will extend the range of human inventions and technical development, to the increase of the productivity of mankind, to the extermination of disease, to the extension of scientific research, to the raising of the standard of physical health, to the sharpening and refinement of the human brain, to the exploitation of the unused and unsuspected resources of the planet, to the prolongation of human life, and to the furtherance of any other agency that can stimulate the intellectual, the moral and spiritual life of the entire human race.

A world federal system, ruling the whole earth and exercising unchallengeable authority over its unimaginably vast resources, blending and embodying the ideals of both the East and the West, liberated from the curse of war and its miseries, and bent on the exploitation of all the available sources of energy on the surface of the planet, a system in which Force is made the servant of Justice, whose life is sustained by its universal recognition of one God and by its allegiance to one common Revelation – such is the goal towards which humanity, impelled by the unifying forces of life, is moving.

'One of the great events', affirms 'Abdu'l-Bahá, 'which is to occur in the Day of the manifestation of that incomparable Branch is the hoisting of the Standard of God among all nations. By this is meant that all nations and kindreds will be gathered together under the shadow of this Divine Banner, which is no other than the Lordly Branch itself, and will become a single nation. Religious and sectarian antagonism, the hostility of races and peoples, and differences among nations, will be eliminated. All men will adhere to one religion, will have one common faith, *will be blended into one race and become a single people. All will dwell in one common fatherland, which is the planet itself.' 'Now, in the world of being,' He has moreover explained, 'the Hand of Divine power hath firmly laid the foundations of this all-highest bounty, and this wondrous gift. Whatsoever is latent in the innermost of this holy Cycle shall gradually appear and be made manifest, for now is but the beginning of its growth, and the dayspring of the revelation of its signs. Ere the close of this century and of this age, it shall be made clear and evident how wondrous was that spring-tide, and how heavenly was that gift.'*[41]

From *The Advent of Divine Justice* (letter to the Bahá'ís of the United States and Canada, 25 December 1938)

Of these spiritual prerequisites of success, which constitute the bedrock on which the security of all teaching plans, Temple projects, and financial schemes, must ultimately rest, the following stand out as preeminent and vital, which the members of the American Bahá'í community will do well to ponder. Upon the extent to which these basic requirements are met, and the manner in which the American believers fulfil them in their individual lives, administrative activities, and social relationships, must depend the measure of the manifold blessings which the All-Bountiful Possessor can vouchsafe to them all. These requirements are none other than a high sense of moral rectitude in their social and administrative activities, absolute chastity in their individual lives, and complete freedom from prejudice in their dealings with peoples of a different race, class, creed, or colour . . .

Such a rectitude of conduct must manifest itself, with ever-increasing potency, in every verdict which the elected representatives of the Bahá'í community, in whatever capacity they may find themselves, may be called upon to pronounce. It must be constantly reflected in the business dealings of all its members, in their domestic lives, in all manner of employment, and in any service they may, in the future, render their government or people. It must be exemplified in the conduct of all Bahá'í electors, when exercising their sacred rights and functions. It must characterize the attitude of every loyal believer towards non-acceptance of political posts, non-identification with political parties, non-participation in political controversies, and non-membership in political organizations and ecclesiastical institutions. It must reveal itself in the uncompromising adherence of all, whether young or old, to the clearly enunciated and fundamental principles laid down by 'Abdu'l-Bahá in His addresses, and to the laws and ordinances revealed by Bahá'u'lláh in His Most Holy Book. It must be demonstrated in the impartiality of every defender of the Faith against its enemies, in his fair-mindedness in recognizing any merits that enemy may possess, and in his honesty in discharging any obligations he may have towards him. It must constitute the brightest ornament of the life, the pursuits, the exertions, and the utterances of every Bahá'í teacher, whether labouring at home or abroad, whether in the front ranks of the teaching force, or occupying a less active and responsible position. It must be made the hall-mark of that numerically small, yet intensely dynamic and highly responsible body of the elected national representatives of every Bahá'í community, which constitutes the sustaining pillar, and the sole instrument for the election, in every community, of that Universal House whose very name and title, as ordained by Bahá'u'lláh, symbolizes that rectitude of conduct which is its highest mission to safeguard and enforce . . .

As to a chaste and holy life it should be regarded as no less essential a factor that must contribute its proper share to the strengthening and vitalization of the Bahá'í community, upon which must in turn depend the success of any Bahá'í plan or enterprise. In these days when the forces of irreligion are weakening the moral fibre, and undermining the foundations of individual morality, the obligation of chastity and holiness must claim an increasing share of the attention of the American believers, both in their individual capacities and as the responsible custodians of the interests of the Faith of Bahá'u'lláh. In the discharge of such an obligation, to which the special circumstances resulting from an excessive and enervating materialism now prevailing in their country lend particular significance, they must play a conspicuous and predominant role. All of them, be they men or women, must, at this threatening hour when the lights of religion are fading out, and its restraints are one by one being abolished, pause to examine themselves, scrutinize their conduct, and with characteristic resolution arise to purge the life of their community of every trace of moral laxity that might stain the name, or impair the integrity, of so holy and precious a Faith.

A chaste and holy life must be made the controlling principle in the behaviour and conduct of all Bahá'ís, both in their social relations with the members of their own community, and in their contact with the world at large. It must adorn and reinforce the ceaseless labours and meritorious exertions of those whose enviable position is to propagate the Message, and to administer the affairs, of the Faith of Bahá'u'lláh. It must be upheld, in all its integrity and implications, in every phase of the life of those who fill the ranks of that Faith, whether in their homes, their travels, their clubs, their societies, their entertainments, their schools, and their universities. It must be accorded special consideration in the conduct of the social activities of every Bahá'í summer school and any other occasions on which Bahá'í community life is organized and fostered. It must be closely and continually identified with the mission of the Bahá'í Youth, both as an element in the life of the Bahá'í community, and as a factor in the future progress and orientation of the youth of their own country.

Such a chaste and holy life, with its implications of modesty, purity, temperance, decency, and clean-mindedness, involves no less than the exercise of moderation in all that pertains to dress, language, amusements, and all artistic and literary avocations. It demands daily vigilance in the control of one's carnal desires and corrupt inclinations. It calls for the abandonment of a frivolous conduct, with its excessive attachment to trivial and often misdirected pleasures. It requires total abstinence from all alcoholic drinks, from opium, and from similar habit-forming drugs. It condemns the prostitution of art and of literature, the practices of nudism and of companionate marriage, infidelity in marital relationships, and all manner of promiscuity, of easy familiarity, and of sexual vices. It can tolerate no compromise with the theories, the standards, the habits, and the excesses of a decadent age. Nay rather it seeks to demonstrate, through the dynamic force of its example, the pernicious character of such theories, the falsity of such standards, the hollowness of such claims, the perversity of such habits, and the sacrilegious character of such excesses.

'By the righteousness of God!' writes Bahá'u'lláh, 'The world, its vanities and its glory, and whatever delights it can offer, are all, in the sight of God, as worthless as, nay even more contemptible than, dust and ashes. Would that the hearts of men could comprehend it. Wash yourselves thoroughly, O people of Bahá, from the defilement of the world, and of all that pertaineth unto it. God Himself beareth Me witness! The things of the earth ill beseem you. Cast them away unto such as may desire them, and fasten your eyes upon this most holy and effulgent Vision . . .'

It must be remembered, however, that the maintenance of such a high standard of moral conduct is not to be associated or confused with any form of asceticism, or of excessive and bigoted puritanism. The standard inculcated by Bahá'u'lláh, seeks, under no circumstances, to deny any one the legitimate right and privilege to derive the fullest advantage and benefit from the manifold joys, beauties, and pleasures with which the world has been so plentifully enriched by an All-Loving Creator. 'Should a man', Bahá'u'lláh Himself reassures us, 'wish to adorn himself with the ornaments of the earth, to wear its apparels, or partake of the benefits it can bestow, no harm can befall him, if he alloweth nothing whatever to intervene between him and God, for God hath ordained every good thing, whether created in the heavens or in the earth, for such of His servants as truly believe in Him.

Eat ye, O people, of the good things which God hath allowed you, and deprive not yourselves from His wondrous bounties. Render thanks and praise unto Him, and be of them that are truly thankful.'

As to racial prejudice, the corrosion of which, for well nigh a century, has bitten into the fibre, and attacked the whole social structure of American society, it should be regarded as constituting the most vital and challenging issue confronting the Bahá'í community at the present stage of its evolution. The ceaseless exertions which this issue of paramount importance calls for, the sacrifices it must impose, the care and vigilance it demands, the moral courage and fortitude it requires, the tact and sympathy it necessitates, invest this problem, which the American believers are still far from having satisfactorily resolved, with an urgency and importance that cannot be over-estimated. White and Negro, high and low, young and old, whether newly converted to the Faith or not, all who stand identified with it must participate in, and lend their assistance, each according to his or her capacity, experience, and opportunities, to the common task of fulfilling the instructions, realizing the hopes, and following the example, of 'Abdu'l-Bahá. Whether coloured or non-coloured, neither race has the right, or can conscientiously claim, to be regarded as absolved from such an obligation, as having realized such hopes, or having faithfully followed such an example. A long and thorny road, beset with pitfalls, still remains untravelled, both by the white and the Negro exponents of the redeeming Faith of Bahá'u'lláh. On the distance they cover, and the manner in which they travel that road, must depend, to an extent which few among them can imagine, the operation of those intangible influences which are indispensable to the spiritual triumph of the American believers and the material success of their newly-launched enterprise.

Let them call to mind, fearlessly and determinedly, the example and conduct of 'Abdu'l-Bahá while in their midst. Let them remember His courage, His genuine love, His informal and indiscriminating fellowship, His contempt for and impatience of criticism, tempered by His tact and wisdom. Let them revive and perpetuate the memory of those unforgettable and historic episodes and occasions on which He so strikingly demonstrated His keen sense of justice, His spontaneous sympathy, for the down-trodden, His ever-abiding sense of the oneness of the human race, His overflowing love for its members, and His displeasure with those who dared to flout His wishes, to deride His methods, to challenge His principles, or to nullify His acts.

To discriminate against any race, on the ground of its being socially backward, politically immature, and numerically in a minority, is a flagrant violation of the spirit that animates the Faith of Bahá'u'lláh. The consciousness of any division or cleavage in its ranks is alien to its very purpose, principles, and ideals. Once its members have fully recognized the claim of its Author, and, by identifying themselves with its Administrative Order, accepted unreservedly the principles and laws embodied in its teachings, every differentiation of class, creed, or colour must automatically be obliterated, and never be allowed, under any pretext, and however great the pressure of events or of public opinion, to reassert itself. If any discrimination is at all to be tolerated, it should be a discrimination not against, but rather in favour of the minority, be it racial or otherwise. Unlike the nations and peoples of the earth, be they of the East or of the West, democratic or authoritarian, communist or capitalist, whether belonging to the Old World or the New, who either ignore, trample upon, or extirpate, the racial, religious, or political minorities within the sphere of their jurisdiction, every organized community enlisted under the banner of Bahá'u'lláh should feel it to be its first and inescapable obligation to nurture, encourage, and safeguard every minority belonging to any faith, race, class, or nation within it. So great and vital is this principle that in such circumstances, as when an equal number of ballots have been cast in an election, or where the qualifications for any office are balanced as between the various races, faiths or nationalities within the community, priority should unhesitatingly be accorded the party representing the minority, and this for no other reason except to stimulate and encourage it, and afford it an opportunity to further the interests of the community. In the light of this principle, and bearing in mind the extreme desirability of having the minority elements participate and share responsibility in the conduct of Bahá'í activity, it should be the duty of every Bahá'í community so to arrange its affairs that in cases where individuals belonging to the divers minority elements within it are already qualified and fulfil the necessary requirements, Bahá'í representative institutions, be they Assemblies, conventions, conferences, or committees, may have represented on them as many of these divers elements, racial or otherwise, as possible. The adoption of such a course, and faithful adherence to it, would not only be a source of inspiration and encouragement to those elements that are numerically small and inadequately represented, but would demonstrate to the world at large the universality and representative character of the Faith of Bahá'u'lláh, and the freedom of His followers from the taint of those prejudices which have already wrought such havoc in the domestic affairs, as well as the foreign relationships, of the nations.

Freedom from racial prejudice, in any of its forms, should, at such a time as this when an increasingly large section of the human race is falling a victim to its devastating ferocity, be adopted as the watchword of the entire body of the American believers, in whichever state they reside, in whatever circles they move, whatever their age, traditions, tastes, and habits. It should be consistently demonstrated in every phase of their activity and life, whether in the Bahá'í community or outside it, in public or in private, formally as well as informally, individually as well as in their official capacity as organized groups, committees and Assemblies. It should be deliberately cultivated through the various and every-day opportunities, no matter how insignificant, that present themselves, whether in their homes, their business offices, their schools and colleges, their social parties and recreation grounds, their Bahá'í meetings, conferences, conventions, summer schools and Assemblies. It should, above all else, become the keynote of the policy of that august body which, in its capacity as the national representative, and the director and coordinator of the affairs of the community, must set the example, and facilitate the application of such a vital principle to the lives and activities of those whose interests it safeguards and represents . . .

A tremendous effort is required by both races if their outlook, their manners, and conduct are to reflect, in this darkened age, the spirit and teachings of the Faith of Bahá'u'lláh. Casting away once and for all the fallacious doctrine of racial superiority, with all its attendant evils, confusion, and miseries, and welcoming and encouraging the intermix-ture of races, and tearing down the barriers that now divide them, they should each endeavour, day and night, to fulfil their particular responsibilities in the common task which so urgently faces them. Let them, while each is attempting to contribute its share to the solution of this perplexing problem, call to mind the warnings of 'Abdu'l-Bahá, and visualize, while there is yet time, the dire consequences that must follow if this challenging and unhappy situation that faces the entire American nation is not definitely remedied.

Let the white make a supreme effort in their resolve to contribute their share to the solution of this problem, to abandon once for all their usually inherent and at times subconscious sense of superiority, to correct their tendency towards revealing a patronizing attitude towards the members of the other race, to persuade them through their intimate, spontaneous and informal association with them of the genuineness of their friendship and the sincerity of their intentions, and to master their impatience of any lack of responsiveness on the part of a people who have received, for so long a period, such grievous and slow-healing wounds. Let the Negroes, through a corresponding effort on their part, show by every means in their power the warmth of their response, their readiness to forget the past, and their ability to wipe out every trace of suspicion that may still linger in their hearts and minds. Let neither think that the solution of so vast a problem is a matter that exclusively concerns the other. Let neither think that such a problem can either easily or immediately be resolved. Let neither think that they can wait confidently for the solution of this problem until the initiative has been taken, and the favourable circumstances created, by agencies that stand outside the orbit of their Faith. Let neither think that anything short of genuine love, extreme patience, true humility, consummate tact, sound initiative, mature wisdom, and deliberate, persistent, and prayerful effort, can succeed in blotting out the stain which this patent evil has left on the fair name of their common country. Let them rather believe, and be firmly convinced, that on their mutual understanding, their amity, and sustained cooperation, must depend, more than on any other force or organization operating outside the circle of their Faith, the deflection of that dangerous course so greatly feared by 'Abdu'l-Bahá, and the materialization of the hopes He cherished for their joint contribution to the fulfilment of that country's glorious destiny.[42]

Notes and References

Chapter 2: Religious Doctrines

1. Bahá'u'lláh, *Gleanings*, XXVI.
2. ibid.
3. Bahá'u'lláh, *Hidden Words*, Arabic nos. 3 and 4.
4. For a discussion of these terms and of Bahá'í theology in general, see Juan Cole, 'The concept of manifestation in the Bahá'í writings', *Bahá'í Studies*, 1982.
5. Bahá'u'lláh, *Hidden Words*, Arabic nos. 11 and 13.
6. 'Abdu'l-Bahá, *Promulgation*, p. 107.

Chapter 3: Social Doctrines

7. Bahá'u'lláh, *Tablets*, p. 129.
8. 'Abdu'l-Bahá, 'Tablet to the Hague', in *Bahá'í Revelation*, p. 208.
9. 'Abdu'l-Bahá, *Secret of Divine Civilization*, pp. 18 and 110.

Chapter 4: Morality and Spirituality

10. 'Abdu'l-Bahá in London, p. 109.
11. Bahá'u'lláh, *Hidden Words*, Arabic no. 9.
12. Bahá'u'lláh, *Tablets*, p. 36.
13. Bahá'u'lláh, *Gleanings*, CXXX.
14. Bahá'u'lláh, *Hidden Words*, Arabic no. 2.
15. 'Abdu'l-Bahá, *Some Answered Questions*, p. 215.
16. Bahá'u'lláh, *Gleanings*, CXXXVI.
17. Shoghi Effendi, *Advent*, pp. 24–8.
18. 'Abdu'l-Bahá, *Will and Testament*, p. 14.
19. Esslemont, *New Era*, p. 99.
20. Bahá'u'lláh, *Hidden Words*, Arabic no. 27.

21. Bahá'u'lláh, *Prayers and Meditations*, CLXXXI.
22. Bahá'u'lláh, *Hidden Words*, Arabic no. 31.
23. 'Abdu'l-Bahá, in *Bahá'í Prayers*, p. 90.
24. Bahá'u'lláh, *Gleanings*, LXX.
25. *Principles*, pp. 90–91.
26. Esslemont, *New Era*, p. 88.

Appendix

27. Bahá'u'lláh, *Hidden Words*, Arabic, introduction, nos. 1, 2, 4, 5, 7, 27, 31, 32, 40, 42, 48, 50, 55, 67, 68; Persian nos. 1, 3, 4, 5, 6, 14, 18, 40, 44, 50, 53, 76.
28. Bahá'u'lláh, *Certitude*, pp. 192–200.
29. *Bahá'í Revelation*, pp. 4–9.
30. ibid., pp. 9–11.
31. Bahá'u'lláh, *Gleanings*, CLV.
32. ibid., CLIX.
33. Bahá'u'lláh, *Tablets*, pp. 124–30.
34. Bahá'u'lláh, *Gleanings*, I.
35. Bahá'u'lláh, *Prayers and Meditations*, IX.
36. ibid., XCIV.
37. 'Abdu'l-Bahá, *Paris Talks*, pp. 15–17, 79–81, 119–23.
38. 'Abdul-Bahá, *Bahá'í Revelation*, pp. 237–40.
39. *Promulgation*, pp. 133–7.
40. 'Abdu'l-Bahá, 'Tablet to the Hague', in *Bahá'í Revelation*, pp. 208–19.
41. Shoghi Effendi, *World Order*, pp. 168–71, 190–91, 202–5.
42. Shoghi Effendi, *Advent*, pp. 18–34.

Bibliography

There is now an extensive Bahá'í literature, including a number of general introductions to the Bahá'í Faith written by Bahá'ís. The most comprehensive of these are John E. Esslemont's *Bahá'u'lláh and the New Era*, with editions produced by the Publishing Trusts of the United Kingdom, India and the United States; John Ferraby, *All Things Made New: A Comprehensive Outline of the Bahá'í Faith*, rev. ed. (Oakham: Bahá'í Publishing Trust, 1987 – also in an Indian edition); William S. Hatcher and J. Douglas Martin, *The Bahá'í Faith: The Emerging Global Religion* (New York: Harper & Row, 1984); and John Huddlestone, *The Earth is But One Country* (London: Bahá'í Publishing Trust, 1976). A more critical and historical account is provided by Peter Smith, *The Babi and Baha'i Religions: From Messianic Shi'ism to a World Religion* (Cambridge: Cambridge University Press, 1986). For an introduction to literature produced by the Bahá'ís, see Eunice Braun, *A Reader's Guide: The Development of Bahá'í Literature in English* (Oxford: George Ronald, 1986).

Many volumes of Bahá'í scripture and other authoritative writings have been published in Persian, Arabic and English. There are also extensive translations in other languages. In English, publications include the following works cited in the present book:

'Abdu'l-Bahá. *Paris Talks: Addresses Given by 'Abdu'l-Bahá in Paris in 1911–1912*. 11th ed. London: Bahá'í Publishing Trust: 1969.

—— *The Promulgation of Universal Peace*. Compiled by Howard MacNutt. 2nd ed. Wilmette, Illinois: Bahá'í Publishing Trust, 1982.

—— *The Secret of Divine Civilization*. Translated by Marzieh Gail. Wilmette, Illinois: Bahá'í Publishing Trust, 1957.

—— *Selections from the Writings of 'Abdu'l-Bahá*. Translated by a Committee at the Bahá'í World Centre and by Marzieh Gail. Haifa: Bahá'í World Centre, 1978.

—— *Some Answered Questions*. Translated by Laura Clifford Barney. Rev. ed. Wilmette, Illinois: Bahá'í Publishing Trust, 1981.

—— *Will and Testament of 'Abdu'l-Bahá*. Wilmette, Illinois: Bahá'í Publishing Trust, 1981.

Bahá'u'lláh. *Gleanings from the Writings of Bahá'u'lláh*. Compiled and translated by Shoghi Effendi. Rev. ed. London: Bahá'í Publishing Trust, 1978.

—— *The Hidden Words*. Rev. ed. London: National Spiritual Assembly of the Bahá'ís of the British Isles, 1932.

—— *The Kitáb-i-Íqán: The Book of Certitude*. Translated by Shoghi Effendi. London: Bahá'í Publishing Trust, 1946.

—— *Prayers and Meditations by Bahá'u'lláh*. Compiled and translated by Shoghi Effendi. Rev. ed. London: Bahá'í Publishing Trust, 1978.

—— *A Synopsis and Codification of the Kitáb-i-Aqdas: The Most Holy Book of Bahá'u'lláh*. Haifa: Bahá'í World Centre, 1973.

—— *Tablets of Bahá'u'lláh revealed after the Kitáb-i-Aqdas*. Compiled by the Research Department of the Universal House of Justice and translated by Habib Taherzadeh with the assistance of a Committee at the Bahá'í World Centre. Haifa: Bahá'í World Centre, 1978.

Shoghi Effendi. *The Advent of Divine Justice*. Rev. ed. Wilmette, Illinois: Bahá'í Publishing Trust, 1963.

—— *God Passes By*, Wilmette, Illinois: Bahá'í Publishing Trust, 1944.

—— *The World Order of Bahá'u'lláh*. Rev. ed. Wilmette, Illinois: Bahá'í Publishing Trust, 1955.

Universal House of Justice. *The Promise of World Peace*. Haifa: Bahá'í World Centre, 1985.

Other books cited:

'Abdu'l-Bahá in London. London: Bahá'í Publishing Trust, 1982.

Bahá'í Prayers. A Selection. London: Bahá'í Publishing Trust, 1975.

The Bahá'í Revelation. London: Bahá'í Publishing Trust, 1955.

Esslemont, John E., *Bahá'u'lláh and the New Era*. 4th ed. London: Bahá'í Publishing Trust, 1974.

Principles of Bahá'í Administration. 3rd ed. London: Bahá'í Publishing Trust, 1973.

Note: Where available, the edition published by the British Bahá'í Publishing Trust has been cited. Editions produced by the American and Indian Bahá'í Publishing Trusts are often also available. With the Bahá'í World Centre in Haifa, these three Publishing Trusts are the main English language publishers of Bahá'í scripture.

LAKEWOOD MEMORIAL LIBRARY
LAKEWOOD, NEW YORK 14750